THE MAGIC OF BALANCED LIVING

HOW TO FIND HEALTH, HAPPINESS, AND SUCCESS IN TODAY'S HIGH-STRESS WORLD

TODD KUPPER RD, LDN
AUTHOR, SPEAKER, ENTREPRENEUR, MARTIAL ARTIST, AND MAGICIAN

The Magic of Balanced Living: How to Find Health, Happiness, and Success in Today's High-Stress World

Acknowledgments

This book has been a lifetime in the making.

And, though I'm the guy with my name on the cover, this book never could have happened without the love and support I've received over the years from my wife and children; family and friends; colleagues; and audiences. In so many ways, this is their book as much as mine.

Yes, I put the words on paper, but they put the ideas in my head. They also gave me the confidence to do what many others said I couldn't. So, I want to thank some of them here.

To my wife, Lisa: Thank you for your love and support, for being my best friend, and for bringing out the very best in me.

To my children, Tommy and Emma: Thank you for bringing me such happiness. You are the joy of my life.

To my parents: Thank you for instilling in me all of the values that have so profoundly, and positively, shaped my life. Thank you, also, for your unyielding support.

To all of my friends and mentors in the worlds of Aikido and magic: Thank you for helping me along in my journey of discovery — and for helping me discover the principles of The Balance Diet.

To Ben and Melissa: Thank you for getting me through college, and for teaching me so much along the way.

To Shuji Maruyama Sensei: Thank you for helping me grow up from a boy to a man — and for making me what I am today.

To all of you: I have been blessed with a wonderful life. Mostly, that's because I've been blessed with each of you. Thank you for making this book possible — and for helping me achieve such a wonderful, balanced life.

Sincerely,
Todd

What would you say if I said I could help you live better?

What would you say if I said I could teach you some basic, common sense, easy-to-implement principles that would allow you to live a happier, more successful, more magical, and more balanced life?

You might think I was crazy. You might assume that I would be asking you to do the impossible — to do things that you might not be able to actually do.

Well, you'd be wrong.

Because I am about to teach you about the five principles of a philosophy that I call The Balance Diet — a philosophy that I believe can help you live better than you've ever lived before.

All you have to do is turn the page.

INTRODUCTION

How My Journey
Can Be Your Journey

I was the fat kid.

I grew up in Burholme, a blue-collar neighborhood in Northeast Philadelphia. It was the kind of place where "health food" meant a cheesesteak with American cheese instead of Cheez Whiz, or maybe light beer instead of the regular stuff. My parents fed me all the super-processed, super-unhealthy stuff that everyone else was eating back in the 1980s: soda, white bread, and potato chips. Breakfast was bacon and eggs, toast slathered with butter, or those super-sugary cereals — you know, the ones with marshmallows.

Other kids could get away with the Burholme diet. I couldn't. By the time I was in high school, my distinguishing characteristic was my weight. I remember the kids calling me "The Pillsbury Dough Boy."

Yeah, I was fat. It never seemed that big a deal to me, though. I wasn't shy. I wasn't a shut-in. I had plenty of friends, and parents who cared. And I did stuff. I played sports. I hung out with my buddies in the neighborhood. Sometimes, my brother and I would try to make some money on the side by helping our uncle hawk shady health food supplements. Yes, I was a fat kid selling health food supplements. But even back then, I could make a sale.

So, no, I didn't think much about my weight, other than to accept that I was fat, and that I would always be fat. That's just the way it was.

I thought I was fine with it.

Then Jenny, my high school girlfriend, broke up with me.

OK, let's pause for a second.

Because I know what you're thinking.

You're thinking that the rest of this book is going to be some sappy weight-loss story. You're thinking that I'm going to tell you about the emotional wreck I was after getting dumped by Jenny (and for the record, no, I didn't see this one coming), and how I decided right then and there to change my life forever. How I decided to swear off every food with any kind of flavor. How I committed myself to working out compulsively, with freakish intensity, and generally living my life by a rigid standard of behavior that you'll never be able to match.

Maybe you're thinking you've heard this story before. Maybe you're thinking The Balance Diet is a sham. Maybe you're thinking that you want to stop reading.

Don't.

Just hang in there with me for just a bit longer.

I promise you this much: This is *not* a weight loss book.

It's not actually a diet book, either, though I am a registered dietitian (more on that later). This is not exactly a self-help guide. And, it's not exactly a memoir. In fact, I'm not sure what it is.

I guess I'll just explain it this way: This is a book about living life — or, maybe more to the point, enjoying life — while still living in reality. There's nothing I will teach you in this book that you can't start doing right now. There's nothing about The Balance Diet that is out of your reach.

This is a book about balance — what it means; how to achieve it; and how it can help you live skinnier, healthier, and, yes, happier lives.

Now, back to high school.

I'm not going to be overly dramatic about this. I won't claim that getting dumped by Jenny was the single most transformative moment of my life, or that everything that has followed in the years since — my training as a nutritionist, my professional sales success, my personal happiness, my wife and kids, my mastery of Aikido, my budding new career as a magician (yes, a magician; again, more on that later) — can be traced directly to that crushing adolescent moment in the halls of Northeast High School.

I'll say this much, though: getting dumped sucked. That's for sure.

And, yeah, it was a wake-up call.

I stand roughly 5 feet, 9 inches tall. And, by the time I was a sophomore in high school, I weighed 230 pounds. Do the math: I was fat.

Still, Jenny and I had dated for about 10 months. That's a lifetime for a couple of high school kids in Northeast Philly. We had some good times, too. She cared about me, and because she cared about me, I could pretend that my bulging waistline was no big deal. I could tell myself that being fat wasn't my *choice*, but rather, quite simply, *the way I was supposed to be.*

That may sound ridiculous, and maybe it is. But remember, I didn't exactly grow up in a health-conscious household, or neighborhood, or health-conscious time for that matter. Bacon and eggs is what everyone in Northeast Philly ate for breakfast, and don't forget the scrapple (for those not familiar, scrapple is a combination of pork scraps that are boiled with cornmeal and shaped into loaves for slicing and frying). It just so happened that all of that breakfast fat stuck to my bones a little better.

Today, we see fat people as ticking time bombs. We know they're susceptible to diabetes, heart disease, strokes, and cancer. We know they live shorter, less enjoyable lives. But back then, back in my old neighborhood, fat people were just fat. I was one of them. My parents didn't seem to care I was fat. Jenny didn't seem to care, either.

So why should I?

Here's the funny thing: Jenny never really explained why she was dumping me. For all I know, it could have been my hair. In fact, I am fairly certain that the entire thing had nothing to do with my weight. The relationship had just run its course. But in the terrible clarity of the moment — "I don't want to be with you anymore" — the weight certainly seemed to be a likely culprit. I think I subconsciously decided that, no matter what Jenny's reasons were, I was simply tired of being fat. And I was going to do something about it.

I would lose 100 pounds in the next year.

There was nothing particularly spectacular or complicated about how I lost all that weight. I just did the things that, even to a high school junior, seemed to make sense.

I ate better. My poor mother must have spent hundreds of dollars on pasta and tuna fish.

I worked out a lot, taking up Aikido at the dojo around the corner — the place where I not only discovered my love for the martial arts, but also would meet Sensei, the man who, I believe, revealed to me the importance of balance.

I refused to give in to temptation. I refused to give in to laziness. I stayed committed to my simple, high school plan: Eat well. Work out.

And the weight just sort of melted way.

Looking back now, of course, I can see that there was a lot more going on during that year than just diet and exercise. With every passing day, with every pound lost, my confidence soared. So did my mood. And it's no coincidence, I don't think, that it was during that transformative year that I discovered two of my great passions, two of the most important elements of my life: I discovered my curiosity about nutrition and human health, and I discovered the martial arts.

I also discovered how important a sense of balance is to healthy and happy living.

I couldn't have known it at the time, but almost by coincidence, I had discovered The Balance Diet.

I've worked with and for a lot of people over the years.

Some of them were just flat-out unsuccessful — terrible at their jobs and terrible at life. Some of them were successful but miserable. Some of them were successful and happy — but dangerously unhealthy. Some of them were just bored with life.

I don't want to brag here. But you know what?

For pretty much all of my adult life, I've managed to be successful. And happy. And healthy. And in love with life. I can't imagine living any other way.

This book is about helping you achieve the same. I don't claim to be perfect. I don't claim to have all the answers. I just know that I'm happy — happier than most other people I know — and I believe The Balance Diet is a big reason why.

So what *is* The Balance Diet?

Well, that's not all that easy to explain. I don't really think of it as a "philosophy." That word seems a bit too weighty. To me, The Balance Diet is, well, plain old common sense. Just like my diet back in high school.

It is a diet built on the following five principles:

1.   The Power of a Positive Mind
2.   Achieving Relaxation and Calmness
3.   Living Healthy and Eating Well
4.   Finding the Magic in Your Life
5.   Understanding That Being Selfish Is OK

We're going to explore all five of these principles later, but for now, all you need to know is this: Quite simply, The Balance Diet is a plan to help you make the most of your life.

I know it's a plan that works, too. Because I've seen it work for me.

The Balance Diet has helped me achieve enormous professional success.

For years now, I've been among the most successful salesmen in my sector. It's been that way from the start, despite the fact that back when I took the job, I'd never held a sales job in my life.

Over the past decade, I've made more money that I ever expected — certainly more than I would have dreamed when I was a kid back in Northeast Philly.

Oh, and I've managed all of this professional success without having to sacrifice my personal life. I wouldn't even think of it.

Besides, put in too many hours and — yep, you guessed it — you're out of balance.

The Balance Diet has helped me achieve a happy home and personal life.

It astounds me how many unhappy people there are in the world. More to the point, it astounds me how many unhappy people there are in my little world.

So many of my friends seem so miserable: miserable with their jobs, miserable in their marriages, miserable with just about every-thing in their lives. *I mean, what's the point?*

So far as we know, we only get one go-around here on Earth. My plan has always been to enjoy my time here as much as possible. And I have.

My wife is my best friend and we spend as much time together as possible — quality time, doing things we love. My kids are the light of my life; I relish every moment with them. Every bedtime story.

Every trip to the park. Every new milestone. My friends offer me support and keep me grounded.

All due respect to the workaholics of the world, but I have to ask: What, really, are you working for?

If you're working to support a family, what's the sense of spending all your time at the office, therefore spending *no actual time* with the ones you are supporting? If you're single and carefree, sure, making money is great. But shouldn't you be making the most of your single years? Shouldn't you use some of that money to travel? To take up a new hobby? To spend time with friends? To do some good in the world?

Life does not happen on a computer screen.

The Balance Diet has helped me achieve good health.

As a registered nutritionist, I could throw a lot of science at you about which foods are healthy, and why. I could talk about calories and fat. I could make eating a lot more complicated than it needs to be.

But that's not what The Balance Diet is all about.

You want to know how I think you can achieve a healthier body? Simple: Use common sense and use balance.

I'm no culinary Nazi. I love to eat. I enjoy having a couple beers with my buddies. There's nothing wrong with loving food. There's nothing wrong with having a drink. But as with anything else in life — and as with anything else in The Balance Diet — eating is all about striking a balance.

Yes, have that luxurious dinner with your wife. Yes, go have a hamburger and beer with your buddies for the game.

Just don't do it all the time.

Is that so difficult?

Achieving a balanced diet is so easy that I can't figure out why so many people can't figure it out. Here are the basics:

• Stock your house with fresh fruits and vegetables.
• Don't eat junk food.
• Definitely don't drink soda (and don't let your kids drink it either).
• Stay away from the overprocessed stuff.
• Avoid "fast food" like the plague.
• In fact, avoid anything remotely close to "fast food"— because, let's face it, "fast food" is barely food at all.

All of us know healthy food when we see it. All of us know junk when we see it. Sometimes, good health and nutrition simply comes down to making the right choice — and then making it again and again and again.

The Balance Diet has helped me make peace with myself — and allowed me to make the most of what I am.

It's important, of course, to spend time with your family. It's important to succeed professionally. It's important to make time for friends.

But you know what? It's also important to make time for yourself. No matter what anyone tells you, there's nothing wrong with taking care of yourself. There's nothing wrong with finding a little peace and quiet, or taking on a new challenge that is all your own. There's nothing wrong with escaping your world, even if for 30 minutes a day, to do whatever you want to do.

I truly believe we all need something outside of work, and outside of family and friends. For me, that something is the martial arts. I discovered Aikido way back in high school, during that turbulent junior year, and in the years since, I've found that my practice has brought me much-needed peace, focus, happiness, and, yes, balance. Today, I am a fifth-degree Aikido black belt. I am one of the youngest people in the world to achieve that distinction.

But that's not what's important to me.

I don't practice Aikido for accolades; indeed, most of my time working on Aikido is spent alone, at the dojo, where there is nobody to impress and nobody to beat. Indeed, one of the greatest lessons I've learned from Aikido is this: Don't compete against others. Compete against yourself.

I don't make any money from Aikido. It hasn't given me the body of a movie star. And so to many people, my time spent on Aikido may seem to be something of a waste of time. What they don't understand, of course, is the balance that Aikido brings to my life. In my practice, I strive for — and often achieve — relaxation, a positive outlook, calmness, and correct posture.

Because of Aikido, I am a better father, a better husband, and a better friend.

Because of Aikido, I am one of the most accomplished salesmen in my sector.

Because of Aikido — more specifically, because of the peaceful time alone that my Aikido practice affords me — I am a happier person. And it is precisely because I am happy, I believe, that I discovered the last element of The Balance Diet: magic.

The Balance Diet has helped me discover the magic in my life — and, no, I don't mean the sleight of hand stuff I perform on stage.

Happy people are curious people. Curious about life. Curious about everything.

When you're happy, every day is an adventure: an opportunity to learn something new, take on a new challenge, and broaden your horizons.

A few years ago, while out on a sales call, I met a mildly cranky old fellow who, despite his gruff demeanor, just happened to be one hell of a magician.

Now, I hadn't thought twice about magic before this. But as soon as that cranky old guy showed me one simple card trick, I was hooked. I knew right then and there I wanted to learn magic, too. Though he wasn't thrilled about it, I convinced the magician to become my magic mentor.

Over the next few months, I immersed myself in magic. I learned as many tricks as I could. I mastered them. At some point, my mentor informed me that he couldn't help me anymore.

"Why not?" I asked.

"Because," he answered, "I've taught you everything I can. It's time for you to take the next step."

More than a few of my friends gave me a hard time about this magic business. "Don't you have enough to do?" they asked. "Why are you wasting your time with that?"

Well, here's why: because I enjoyed it. Because it was a challenge. And ... well, *why not?* Is it really that difficult to pick up a deck of cards and learn a trick or two? What else should I be doing with my time? Watching some horrible reality show on television?

My discovery of magic — my commitment to it — has paid dividends in two distinct ways.

First, from a strictly pragmatic perspective, it's made me quite a bit of money. After becoming comfortable with my magic skills — comfortable enough, at least, to perform in front of an audience — I came up with an act that blended my love for magic with my knowledge of nutrition. It's called "The Magic of Nutrition," and I now perform it for schools throughout the Philadelphia region. I wrote a children's book, *The Magic of Breakfast*, around the same idea. I've even been offered a featured role in a new television series about health and nutrition.

But magic has done more than simply sweeten my bank account.

Like Aikido, magic has also enriched my life very much. It's provided a challenge. It's focused my thoughts. It's pushed my brain. It's pushed me. It's brought me wonderment, joy, laughter — and balance.

Ours is a work-a-day, stick-to-the-routine world. We get up, we go to work, we sit in front of a computer all day, we come home, we eat dinner, we watch television, and then we go to bed. Then the next day, we do it all again. It's mind-numbing, is what it is. Especially for those of us with families and mortgages and responsibilities and worries, life can at times seem like a slog, rather than a joyride. Responsibilities. Commitments. Problems.

But think back, if you can, to when you were a kid. Think back to a time when the world was a mystery. When magic was all around you.

Remember how wonderful that was?

Well, I'm here to tell you: You can have that feeling again. Magic *is* all around you. And once you achieve balance — once you embrace the simple, common-sense elements of The Balance Diet — I am certain you will feel it.

CHAPTER 1

Balance, and Why It Matters

I am an optimist.

My friends kid me about my enthusiasm sometimes, but I admit this much is true: I wake up every morning truly excited about the possibilities of the day ahead. With good reason, I think. Because no matter how structured or how predictable our lives become — and in this modern world, yes, they can become awfully predictable — the fact is we never really know what awaits us with each new day.

My life is proof of that.

The Balance Diet is proof of that.

Let's go back to high school for a moment.

After Jenny and I broke up, a void opened that, at least subconsciously, I must have set out to fill. I was looking for *something*. I just didn't know what. And I certainly didn't think the something I was looking for would be found right around the corner.

I'm not sure if it would be accurate to say that I "found" Aikido. I think it probably found me. Because the fact is, one random day back in my junior year — a day that started out just like any other — I woke up, went out into the streets of Burholme, and finally took notice of the martial arts studio right there on Rising Sun Avenue. I don't know why I hadn't noticed it before. I don't know why it caught my attention that day, or why I felt the need, all of a sudden, to investigate it further. To be honest, I am fairly certain I didn't have a clue what Aikido was. But it *sounded* cool, at least.

Later that day, when I met up with my buddy Karl for another day of doing whatever it was we did back in those days in Burholme, I told him all about the dojo I had seen over on Rising Sun. An Aikido dojo — right there on Rising Sun Avenue. *I mean, we had an Aikido dojo in Burholme.* This certainly didn't seem like something you'd expect to find in Northeast Philly. To Karl and me, it seemed exotic. Different. Challenging. It was just too mysterious for two high school juniors to pass up.

So we made a pact: Together, we'd find out what Aikido was all about. We'd become Burholme's very own Bruce Lees. We would sign up for Aikido classes.

And man, I was excited.

I had found something to take my mind off all of that other stuff that had been so long weighing me down — literally and figuratively. Aikido was going to save me. I just knew it.

Karl, apparently, did not feel the same.

Now, I'm certainly not perfect. I've never claimed to be. But, I'll say this much for myself: When I say I'm going to do something, I do it. I don't make promises that I can't keep. I don't commit to anything I don't think I can accomplish. When I say I'm going to do something, I do it. I've always been that way.

I don't want to bust on Karl here. Really, I don't. He was a good guy. Still is.

I mean, maybe he didn't have any interest in Aikido in the first place. Maybe he just agreed to sign up in order to appease me (my enthusiasm, as my friends have learned, can be difficult at times to dampen). Or maybe in the hours after we agreed to meet up at the dojo, Karl found something else he wanted to pursue. I don't really know what happened to Karl.

All I know is, when I arrived at the dojo that night to begin my Aikido training, Karl wasn't there.

I was all alone, out front of the dojo, and I had a decision to make: stay or go.

I stayed.

It was one of the best decisions of my life.

By walking into that studio, I not only committed myself to Aikido. I also made a statement about who I wanted to be. I took the first step toward an understanding of balance — and how achieving it can make life better.

Shuji Maruyama Sensei is not a big man. He stands just over 5-feet, 4-inches tall. He might weigh in at 130 pounds. But in the world of Aikido, he is a giant.

There might be five other men in the entire world who are as accomplished at anything as Sensei is at Kokikai Aikido; this really shouldn't be any surprise, given that he's the guy who invented it.

Most of you don't know much about Aikido — all the technical things that separate a *very good* practitioner of the martial art from a true master like Sensei — but let me make this very simple for you: Even now, in his 70s, Sensei can do things that most everyone else on the planet cannot. If he were attacked on the street by a guy the size of an NFL offensive lineman, I am fairly certain Sensei would throw the guy aside without so much as breaking a sweat. So, yeah, that small stature can be deceiving.

Sensei is not a violent man. And Kokikai Aikido is not a violent martial art. But you can be certain of this: Sensei is no man to be trifled with — this goes for both physically and philosophically. I learned that soon enough.

I was just a kid when I met Sensei — more specifically, a somewhat miserable high school kid looking for guidance. A confused, lonely kid looking for something to latch onto. Aikido very quickly became that thing. Which makes sense, I suppose: I mean, I had found Aikido at just the right time.

I'll be honest. I didn't really like high school. More accurately, I hated it. The classroom politics. The endless struggle to be "popular" and "accepted." The jocks. The nerds. The suffocating atmosphere of those cramped halls. And, more than anything else, all of those struggles I had to endure just to get by with passing grades. Ah, the memories.

Believe me, I am a hard worker. Always have been. But I would be lying if I said it didn't bother me when I saw my classmates pulling down A's on tests after studying for just an hour or not at all, while I would study for a week and pray to get a C. It's a cliché, I suppose, but in my case it's true: I'm not a good test-taker. I'm not really good at school. I'm more of a "doer." Put a hurdle in front of me, I'll clear it. Issue me a challenge, I'll meet it. Give me a job to handle, I'll get it done. But school, well, that didn't make sense to me. It wasn't a job. I'm good at jobs.

That's why, at first, I think I approached Aikido like a job. A five-day-a-week, show-up-and-get-it-done job. I got hooked on Aikido right away. So it wasn't long after I first signed up that I began showing up at the dojo almost every single day. Aikido was fascinating to me — it has a unique mix of self-defense and self-improvement. The moves were graceful. The history was interesting. The workouts were challenging. And every day, I felt I made progress. I was getting it.

So, of course, I wanted to learn more. I wanted to be better. Oh yeah, I wanted to lose that weight, too. I was a man on a mission: I was going to make my life better, and I was going to do it through Aikido. And so I decided that I would spend almost every free moment at the dojo.

But, Sensei would have none of it.

And this is why the man is genius.

For the first several weeks of my time at the dojo, Sensei let me do what I wished. I came every day and did my work. He offered support. He taught me and encouraged me, but never pushed me. Not once. Of course, he didn't need to: I was hooked.

I started hanging around more and more. I mean, I lived at that dojo. My family didn't have enough money to pay for all of those lessons, so Sensei let me "pay" my bill by helping out around the dojo. I was one of the first to show up each morning and stuck around late to help Sensei clean up at night.

I never felt comfortable in the halls of my high school. But that dojo — well, it felt like a second home. And Sensei became a second father to me. A mentor, a life coach, and an inspiration. When I was at the dojo, training under Sensei, I felt like I was part of something. I felt, honestly, that I was well on my way to becoming an Aikido master. I felt as though I was making Sensei proud.

And I figured I could just keep it up forever. I figured that, by pouring myself into Aikido, all of my problems, and all of that extra weight, would simply melt away.

Then one day Sensei sat me down and said I had to stop.

I am not sure if it would be accurate to say that Aikido changed my life.

But that conversation certainly did.

Before I tell you what Sensei told me that day, I suppose I should tell you a bit more about Sensei himself — he is a great man, and I wish more people knew more about him.

Sensei came of age at a tough time in his native Japan. The post-World War II years weren't good ones for Japan or its people. While America experienced a boomtime in the 1950s, Japan struggled for survival. The nation was broke. Its people were grief-stricken, shamed, and impoverished. There was little food, little opportunity, and little hope.

Sensei found salvation — or at least distraction — in the martial arts. He took up Aikido.

In so doing, he also (unwittingly) took up a training regimen that he would find to be infinitely more harsh, and less forgiving, than the one he would later offer to his students. Aikido is ultimately a defensive martial art; it's not something you learn in order to attack others.

Nonetheless, Sensei found that his early training days were filled mostly by older, more experienced boys cleaning his clock. (There was a lot of anger in those days in Japan; Sensei believes the people took it out on each other.) The days were long and hard, and the bruises were many. But Sensei persevered. He became one of the best in his country. But I think he also must have resolved early on to change Aikido for the better.

He got that chance in the mid-1960s. Sensei was sent by his sensei back in Japan to teach Aikido in, of all places, Cleveland, Ohio.

Sensei was excited about the opportunity to spread his beloved martial art — a martial art that was as much about peace of mind as self-defense — to a new country. He quickly found out, however, that Americans did not understand Aikido. He also discovered that, to Americans raised on kung-fu movies, all martial arts were about one thing: fighting.

Sensei would spend the next two years changing people's minds, or at least trying to.

I am guessing that even Sensei would tell you those two years in Cleveland didn't go as well as he had hoped. The cultural divide between Japan and the American Midwest, at least back then, was just too wide. He looked at Aikido one way; his students looked at it in another way. For two years while in Cleveland, he dealt with one constant problem: His "students" at the dojo didn't want to learn from him; they wanted to challenge him.

Though Sensei didn't understand this at first, he eventually realized Americans were simply different than the Japanese, and that the two cultures would never completely see eye-to-eye on Aikido. In Japan, masters like Sensei were treated with deference and respect. In America, they were treated as objects — objects to be conquered. As Sensei learned, his American students believed they needed to beat the best in order to be the best.

Sensei didn't agree, and he certainly wasn't going to change his view of Aikido.

But he is a smart man and a realist, too, so he was willing to adjust.

When his contract in Cleveland was up, he headed to Philadelphia. He was a grown man at this point — a mature man, a worldly man — and, in the years that followed, he would make another transformative discovery.

That discovery was *Kokikai.*

Kokikai was a new kind of Aikido — and Sensei was the man who created it. In so doing, he was effectively breaking away from the Aikido establishment — not to mention his own mentors back in Japan. But he was confident that this new Aikido was needed. He was confident that it had something to offer. He was confident it would find an audience. He was right: Today, Kokikai Aikido is taught in 18 different U.S. states and dozens of countries around the world, and Sensei is revered by students everywhere.

So what exactly is Kokikai?

Well, it's a "modern" martial art. Sensei designed it in such a way as to make his students "stronger" — not only physically stronger, but also mentally stronger — and more capable of dealing with the challenges of our too-crazy, too-busy, and too-modern world. It is a martial art that doesn't pit the individual against an opponent, but rather against him or herself. Kokikai's four main principles — calmness, relaxation, good posture, and positivity — are not intended to develop men into warriors. They are intended to help men become better men, and women become better women. The practice of Kokikai may make you tougher to beat in a street fight, but that's not what's important. What's important is that Kokikai will make you a better person. A happier person. A more balanced person. That's precisely what Kokikai has done for me.

Or, maybe more specifically, that's what Sensei did for me.

Because while I saw Aikido as my salvation — my way out of my high school misery — Sensei was the one who told me I was wrong. Sensei was the one who told me that I needed less Aikido, not more.

It couldn't have been an easy conversation for Sensei.

He had to know how much I loved the dojo, how much I loved training. He had to know that I was just a confused kid looking for something to grasp onto — and that I was pretty sure Aikido was that something. He had to know that, given the choice, I would have just kept showing up at the dojo every day. He had to know I needed an escape, and that the dojo was it.

But Sensei had committed his life to turning boys into men. And, as he himself learned back in his early days in Japan, the process of growing up isn't always easy. There are bumps and bruises for all of us. Maybe not all of them are physical. But they are scars nonetheless, and they hurt.

I forget how long it was after I started visiting the dojo that Sensei sat me down. Maybe a couple months or so. I think maybe Sensei wanted to nip the whole thing in the bud. He wanted to get me on the right path as soon as possible — the path to true happiness — and he knew it wasn't a path I was likely to find if I never left his sight.

Do you know what Sensei told me that day? I guess in modern terms, you might say that his message was: *Get a life, Todd.*

Of course, he was far gentler than that. Far more eloquent. But, that was the gist of it.

"Go. Go out," he told me. "Go be with your friends. Go make new friends. Go read a book. You can't spend all your time here. It's not good for you. Life is out there, not in here."

"I want to keep practicing," I told him.

"I want you to keep practicing, too," he said. "Just not every night. Don't plan to come here every night for the rest of your life."

"So how much should I train?

"One night," he said, "for the rest of your life."

And so that was that.

Sensei never actually kicked me out of the dojo. He never locked the doors on me, because he never had to. Though there were days when, more than anything else, I just wanted to hang out at the dojo, go through my training and enjoy my escape, Sensei's message had been delivered. Loud and clear.

A glance from across the room was all that was needed; he would tell me with his eyes, "Life is out there, not in here."

I had no choice but to believe him. And wouldn't you know it? He was right.

That conversation in the dojo — the day Sensei woke me up to the possibilities of the entire world, not just the world inside the dojo — planted inside me the seeds of The Balance Diet. Today, I continue my Aikido practice. I'm really quite good, too. Not as good as Sensei, but pretty good.

Here's the thing, though: I have more than *just* Aikido.

I also have my career. I have my magic. I have my friends, my wife, my family. I have a *life*. It's a balanced life, too — specifically because I haven't spent the last 30 years locked up in some dojo. I have lived my life to the fullest. Aikido has helped me along in my journey, but it has not been the journey itself.

Throughout the rest of this book, I will talk a lot about Aikido, and for obvious reasons: My practice of Aikido has helped me become the man I am today, and helped crystallize in my mind the ideas that have made this book possible.

But here's the thing I want you to understand: *You don't need to practice Aikido to understand The Balance Diet.*

I may have only discovered The Balance Diet because of my time in the dojo. But the ideas behind it are universal. They can make a difference in anyone's life — including your life.

I really believe that.

Starting in the next chapter, I'll explain how.

CHAPTER 2

The Power
of the Positive Mind

There were a lot of reasons why I felt so at home at the dojo.

I loved the camaraderie. I loved learning from Sensei. I loved the challenge of each and every workout — and the great feelings of accomplishment and fulfillment that came with the successful completion of each of my lessons. If I were to be completely honest, though, I'd have to say the *biggest* reason I loved the dojo was this: It was the most positive place I'd ever been. The most encouraging place. The most nurturing place. The most uplifting place.

To be completely honest, I can't recall a *single* negative word being spoken to anyone, ever, at that dojo. I don't think Sensei would have allowed it.

It was the unspoken rule of his dojo: None of his students were ever to be put down. None of his students were ever to be insulted, mocked, or teased. When we walked into Sensei's dojo, we were greeted with a warm welcome. As we trained, we were bombarded with positive feedback. And before we left for the night, we were given an encouraging pat on the back. We were told, very simply: "You did a nice job today."

It may not seem like much. Trivial, even. But believe me, it made a difference.

Through his unique leadership style — a style we all can and should emulate — Sensei created an environment that literally brought out the best in *everybody* who stepped inside. Or, at the very least, brought out the best in everyone who put in the effort. Sensei didn't believe he could turn all of his students into Aikido masters. But he did believe he could make each student as good as he or she could possibly be, given individual abilities.

You know what? *That's exactly what he did.*

I remember the precise moment when I figured this out — when I realized how Sensei measured our accomplishments in that dojo, and how he got each of us to reach our full potential.

It was just another day in the dojo. I had just finished my workout when I noticed a group of students across the room. They weren't my peers, really. At least I didn't think so, because they weren't really on my level — which is why I was so surprised to see them wearing black belts. Now, mind you, I hadn't achieved my black belt yet. This, even though I knew I was better than them, even though I knew they couldn't take me down and even though I knew I could beat them — easily.

I couldn't help myself. I asked Sensei to explain.

"Sensei," I asked, "How come that guy has his black belt?"

Sensei considered my question, and then calmly answered.

"Todd, ask yourself this: Are they better at Aikido today than they were when they first came in here?"

"Yes, Sensei."

"Are they more relaxed today than when they first came in here?"

"Yes."

"Are they more positive?"

"Yes," I answered. "I suppose so."

Sensei nodded. "They are black belts," he said, "because they have done the best they can based on their ability. They deserve black belts because they achieved all they can achieve."

In a way, Sensei had turned the entire American martial arts model — at least, the one that most other dojos I visited used — right on its head. In his wonderful little dojo, he asked us to focus not on what we couldn't control — our height, our weight, our natural athletic ability, our troubles out in the real world — but rather on the things we could: getting better every day, and keeping our Positive Mind intact, even when we struggled. Sensei didn't ask us to beat each other; he asked us to beat our own self-doubts, and our own negativity.

That's what those blackbelts had done. That's what, eventually, I would do, too. Sensei wasn't just teaching us about Aikido. He was teaching us about life — and how to approach it the right way. The fact that he succeeded with all of us — the fact that he made each and every one of us the very best we could be, no matter our limitations — had everything to do, I think, with his endlessly positive attitude. Ultimately, he convinced us to believe in ourselves and to remain, at all times, in a state of Positive Mind.

In the dojo. In the classroom. At work. At home.

What we learned from Sensei was that thinking positive — expecting the best, and not the worst — is at least half the battle. If you believe in something, Sensei taught us, *you really can achieve it*. Nothing was beyond our reach, he told us, if we could simply convince ourselves that it was possible.

Years later, I'm still living by the rules he taught me — and I'm much happier for it.

So are my kids, my wife, my friends, and my employees.

I'll be honest: I've never found *any place* quite as positive as Sensei's dojo. Heck, maybe there is no such place.

But I think I've gone ahead and done the next best thing: I've done whatever I can do to create a life for myself — at home, at the office, and out in the world — that is every bit as positive and nurturing as the dojo was back in my high school days. Through good times and bad, struggles and successes, wins and losses, I've always done my best to remain as positive as possible. I've always reminded myself of the power of a Positive Mind. And I'm happier for it.

In fact, I believe all of my successes — both at home and at work — can be traced back, at least in part, to the fact that I made a conscious decision, years ago, to be a happy, positive person, and not a cynical, depressive one.

It may sound like a cliché, but I believe it's the God's honest truth: Thinking positive can make a difference in your life — and the lives of the people you share your life with.

That's why embracing the power of a Positive Mind is the first key step toward fully achieving a balanced life — and understanding The Balance Diet.

Having a Positive Mind can make you happier.

It can make you more successful, and make the people who work for you more successful, too.

It can make you a better spouse, a better parent, a better friend, and a better boss.

It can make your life more enjoyable, more fulfilling and more full of love.

It can make you look at every day like a gift.

It's so *simple* to achieve, too, this Positive Mind.

So here's a question. *Why are so many of us so miserable?*

Why do we slog our way through our days with such a sense of dread? Why do we spread negativity when we could just as easily spread positivity? Why do we always expect the worst, rather than hope for the best?

Why don't we give ourselves a chance at success?

Seriously, think about those questions for a couple of minutes. Think about how deeply entrenched negativity seems to be in our society — in our workplaces, in our schools, and in our homes. Think about all of the unhappy people you deal with every day — your parents, your friends, your boss, or your coworkers — and then think about how *their* negativity has impacted your life. Think about how easy it can be for a depressed or miserable person to make you depressed or miserable.

Now think how easy it would be for you to stop the cycle. Think how easy it would be for you to be a positive influence on others.

Think how wonderful it would be to live every day with a sense of *wonder*. To see the magic all around you. To wake up in the morning expecting to do great things — and then go to bed at night having *done* those great things.

Think how great it would be to live each day happy, instead of miserable.

When I first got out of college and began my career as a dietitian, I had the great luck to find a great job at a great hospital.

I was excited about that job, too, and ready to make a positive impact with the degree I had worked so hard to achieve. Unfortunately for me, I wound up working for one of the single most miserable, unhappy, and untrusting people I've ever had to deal with. And it wasn't long before she sucked all the joy out of my professional life.

Now, I may have been a young kid at the time and I may have been short on experience, but I also had a degree. It was a degree I had worked toward for four long years and earned at The Pennsylvania State University. I guess my point is this: Yeah, I was a newbie, but I also knew what I was doing. I wanted to excel at my job and do well in my field.

My boss just wouldn't let me.

She didn't trust me to do my job. Heck, she didn't even trust me to work a full eight hours a day. She wanted to know precisely when I got to work, and precisely when I left. She never offered an encouraging word. She never once said, "Good job." She never said much of anything, except to tell me what I was doing wrong. I'll tell you this much: If Sensei's studio was the most positive place in the world, well, my boss' office was the exact opposite — it was the place where positive went to die.

Fortunately, I eventually got out of there before she could crush my positive attitude. And thank God for that, because today, I have people working for me. And, I just don't think I could live with myself if I knew I was being as tough on them as she was on me. I would be miserable knowing I was making others so darn miserable.

Unfortunately, I've been around long enough to know that bosses like me aren't necessarily the norm these days. No, the norm, unfortunately, is to be negative. Judgemental. Untrusting. The norm is to treat your employees like children — to assume that, if you don't constantly beat on them, they'll run around and screw off and not get anything done. And if you're an executive? Well, it seems the norm for those folks is to treat everyone with disdain — to treat their low-level staffers almost as if they're not worthy of their time, or their attention. From what I've seen, these execs seem to enjoy treating the rest of us as if we're not as good as them — and never will be.

I don't know how or why things got this way, but it seems pretty clear to me that, today, it's become almost uncool to be an optimist; to treat staff with respect and kindness; to expect them to achieve great things; and to say, "You did a nice job today."

Nope, only the cynics are hip these days. Only the cutthroat businessmen can succeed. And only the "tough" bosses can get results.

But here's what I'd like to know: What has all of this toughness and negativity really gotten us? Have we *really* achieved anything?

I'll tell you what it's gotten us — a whole lot of unhappiness.

Here's the thing, though.

You don't *have* to follow the norm. You don't *have* to be negative. You don't *have* to walk around waiting for the worst to happen.

You can choose to be happy — because you can choose to have a Positive Mind. You can make this choice every day. Every minute of every day, in fact.

Look, I know it's not easy. I know life can be stressful, especially in these crazy times.

Work. Kids. The mortgage. Deadlines. Health problems. It can wear you down ... quickly. But here's what I'm telling you: *You can't let that happen.* You can't let the stuff you can't control impact the one thing you can control: your attitude.

You are completely in control of the way you live your life, and the way you approach it. So make the right choice: Choose to live happy.

That's what I've done, in part, because that's what I learned from Sensei. But, it's also because of what I learned from my parents.

My folks worked hard. They worked really hard. And though they never had a lot of money — though they still don't have a lot of money today — they've never let what they don't have get in the way of appreciating what they do have: each other; me and my brother; their friends; a roof over their heads; and food on the table.

My father didn't have much of a mother and my mother didn't have much of a father. They could have let that change the way they treated us, but they didn't. They treated me and my brother like gold. My mother spoiled us as best she could, given her budgetary constraints. My father always was, and still is, my best friend. Even when times were tough, they found time for us, and for each other. And, these days, they make sure to find time for their grandchildren.

Throughout their life together, they've always found the courage to look past their problems — and simply live happily.

We all have the same choice.

When we wake up in the morning, we can either decide to look forward to the day to come — to look forward to all of the wonderful opportunities that lay before us — or we can proceed with dread, worry, and fear. Yeah, it sounds simple. Maybe a little bit too simple. But when you really think about it, I'm telling you, it really is that simple.

It all comes down to choices — choices you can make about the way you want to live your life, the way you want to look at the world, and the way you want to be seen by others. And, yes, they are enormous choices.

But here's the good news: They are easy choices to make.

• **You can choose to be a positive person, or you can choose to be a negative person.** It is the most fundamental choice that we face as human beings. And given that simple choice — that simple black-and-white, night-and-day choice — why on Earth would you *choose* to be negative? It just wouldn't make any sense. We get one go-around down here, so, we might as well be happy while we're here.

• **You can choose to surround yourself with positive people, or you can choose to surround yourself with negative people.** I decided a long time ago that I don't have any use for negative people. They bore me. They're trouble, too. Try sharing your goals and ambitions and dreams with a negative person sometime. I guarantee you they'll spend the next hour telling you why you can't achieve them. Believe me, I know. I've been through that. Negative people are a waste of your time. So don't associate with them.

• **You can choose to be a positive influence on others, or you can choose to be a negative influence.** Think about this last one, because this is where the power of a Positive Mind can really make a difference. Because when you make this choice, you're making a choice about the kind of impact you want to have on the world. You're making a choice about the very legacy you'll leave behind — for your family, for your neighborhood, and for your company.

I know you're thinking: That's some weighty stuff. But let me break it down for you here, because, again, it's very simple.

You can either be the kind of boss that people respect, or the kind they fear (and, quite possibly, hate). You can be the kind of parent that your kids trust, or the kind they want to hide from. You can be the kind of person people want to be around, or the kind they avoid.

Of course, we all want to be respected. We all want to be trusted. We all want to be loved. But those things cannot be achieved through money or fame or power.

They can only be achieved through the Power of a Positive Mind.

CHAPTER 3

Relaxation & Calmness: The Difficult But Essential Keys to The Balance Diet

A recent study by the Nielsen Company — the folks who do the television ratings — showed that the average American now spends more than eight hours every day staring at some kind of "screen."

Television screens, of course, take up a couple of those hours. But the rest of it? Yep, you guessed it: computer screens and cell-phone screens. BlackBerries, iPods, and smartphones. We check e-mail, send text messages, and troll the Internet at home, even though we just spent all day at work trolling the Internet.

Americans are addicted to information. And, we're also addicted to work.

Here's a question for you: How often do you get home from work at night, walk into your home, and greet your family after being out and about all day ... and then *immediately* check your BlackBerry — just to make sure you didn't miss any "important" e-mails? How many hours do you spend, on your weekends, parked in front of your laptop, catching up on work or paying bills? When you are "away from work," how much time are you actually *away from work*?

If you're completely honest with yourself, I'd guess that you'll come up with the same answer most people will come up with these days: not enough.

There's no question, ours is a workaholic society, and the rise of technology has made many great things possible — we have immediate access to every bit of information we desire and we can reach just about anybody we want, just about anytime we wish. However, that technology is also robbing us of something more important: our time to simply sit back, check out from reality, and, for once, relax.

Yes, that's right. Just … *relax*.

I mean, just think about this for a second. We, as a society, are working so hard, and doing so much, and multitasking so often, that we rarely even take the time anymore to enjoy the fruits of our labor. Our culture has put a premium on money and success, and certainly there's nothing wrong with striving to do the best you can, financially and otherwise, for your family.

There's nothing wrong with working hard, either.

But I'm telling you, if you don't take a timeout now and again — if you can't make yourself mentally check out for a few minutes every single day — you're setting yourself up for trouble.

Big trouble.

Relaxation.

It's a word that gets tossed around a lot. But I don't think we as a society truly understand what the word actually means anymore. And we certainly don't understand how to achieve it.

Here's my take on what the general public thinks relaxation is: Sitting on the couch, wolfing down potato chips, vegging out in front of the television, getting fat, feeling like a slug, and passing the hours and dreading the next day of work.

I'm sorry, but that's not true relaxation. It's not that kind of relaxation I want you to try and achieve, and it's not the kind of relaxation that I believe is so crucial — central, even — to The Balance Diet.

Let's be honest, if you spend your *entire workday* sitting in front of a computer screen and then spend your *entire evening* staring at your television screen, you're most definitely not finding relaxation. You're just making the subtle switch from ingesting work-related information to ingesting non-work-related information. You're just putting your brain on autopilot — shutting it down, staring at the TV, and zoning out from reality, but not necessarily doing it any good.

The relaxation I want you to think about is a bit more complicated than that. It's a bit more involved, but a great deal more relaxing. And, it's more productive, too.

I'll tell you how to achieve this kind of relaxation — or, at the very least, how you can try to achieve it — in just a moment, but first, I have to pass along the following two pieces of information.

1. Relaxation and calmness are the most *important* elements of The Balance Diet.
2. Relaxation and calmness also are the most *difficult* elements of The Balance Diet to achieve.

Believe me. That second statement is true, very true. I know this better than anyone. Because as far as I've come over the years — as much progress as I've made in achieving happiness, success, and balance in my life — there is nothing I struggle with more than achieving relaxation, than finding a sense of calmness.

I am what you might call a "go-getter." I'm always on the move. I'm always making plans. I'm always looking for the *next* challenge. I can't tell you how many times my friends and family have told me, "Todd, just relax, will ya?" See, while this whole go-getter thing is one of my greatest strengths, it's also one of my greatest weaknesses. Maybe my greatest weakness, period. If there's one thing a go-getter isn't good at, it's turning that go-getting off.

For me, and for people like me, it's very hard — almost impossible sometimes — to shut things down and to take a breath ... to smell the roses, as they say. It's so hard, because there's always that nagging voice in our heads, tsk-tsking us for our "laziness." "Isn't there something else you could be doing?" the voice nags. "Isn't there something else you *should* be doing?"

I have to admit, I listen to that voice more than I should. The reason is obvious: The voice has done me plenty of good over the years. It got me through school. It got me in shape. It made me a successful businessman. It probably made me a better magician, too.

But when I listen to that voice too often, and when I go and go and go for too long, you know what happens? I lose my balance.

I become a less connected and caring father. A less supportive manager. A less productive salesman. A less happy person.

The voice can get me to do a lot of things, and a lot of those things are good. The problem is, however, that there's one major thing it *won't* let me do: Relax.

That's why I've spent years trying to find ways to block that voice out, at least every once in a while. And you know what? I'm getting better at it.

Relaxation is hard to achieve today, maybe more than ever before.

As we've discussed in previous chapters, ours is a busy, hectic world. We have been programmed to run, run, and run some more. But if you run too hard and for too long, you're going to run out of steam. You're going to collapse, break down, and burn out.

The bottom line? You can't run forever. And you know what? Even if you could, I still don't think it would be a *good idea*. Because let's be honest: We were not put on this Earth to stare at a computer screen all day, answer e-mails at 11:00 p.m., fret over our 401(k) statements, or worry about every little thing under the Sun.

We were put on this Earth to live a life. And, why not make sure we're living a *good* life?

Why not make sure we're enjoying the fruits of our labor? Why not take a step back once in a while, sit out under the stars, stare up at the sky and count our blessings? Why not spend 30 minutes a day simply reflecting on our good fortune — our children; our families and friends; the good times we've had; the many gifts we've been given? Why not simply take a deep breath, each and every morning, and think to ourselves: "Today is going to be a great day, and I am thankful for it."

Maybe you think I'm talking about "meditation" here. And, hey, maybe I am. Meditation is a wonderful thing, and savvy doctors — not to mention generations of people who have happily practiced it — will tell you that this age-old method produces results like happiness, serenity, peace, relaxation, and calmness.

But here's the thing: I don't believe that meditation can *only* be practiced in a yoga studio. I don't think you need extensive training in the art of meditation to do it right. I don't believe its benefits are beyond your reach just because you've never tried it before.

What I do believe is that the central idea behind meditation — that concerted striving for clarity, calmness, and a sense of stress-free living, holds benefits for all of us, *enormous benefits*.

If you can achieve a sense of relaxation once a day, even for a short time, and if you can find a steady calmness to carry you through life's storms, you will be well on your way to a life of happiness — and a life of balance.

When I was in high school, just around the time of those life-

changing experiences of my sophomore year, my father was diag-
nosed with cancer.

It was a horrible time for my family — a stressful time for my
brother and my mom and me; and a scary time for my father, a
strong man who always seemed somewhat indestructible to me. It's a
cliché, of course, but it's true: When you're a kid, you just sort of go
about your business assuming your parents are always going to be
there. When you're finally confronted with the reality that they won't
be, well, that's a tough pill to swallow.

I'll be honest, I don't want to spend too much time talking about
that time of my life. I don't want to recount my dad's illness, or talk
about how it changed life in my house back there in Northeast Philly.

What I do want to point out is that my dad's sickness (and, yes,
his eventual recovery) arrived, coincidentally, at just about the same
time that I discovered Aikido. And I believe deeply to this day that
my practice of Aikido — a martial art that preaches constantly of the
crucial importance of relaxation and calmness — helped me weather
that storm.

As I've written in earlier chapters, The Balance Diet isn't only for
people who practice the martial arts. You don't need to take up
Aikido to do the Diet right. But, I do believe the lessons of Eastern
culture generally, and Aikido specifically, hold valuable lessons for
our all-too-crazed Western culture.

Among the greatest lessons — maybe the greatest of all — is that
enlightenment and peace can only come to those who achieve relaxation, to those who can live with a sense of calmness.

Imagine me again, just for a second, as that portly, unhappy,
overly anxious high school sophomore — the kid with the weight of
the world on his shoulders because of his recent breakup, because
of his unhappiness at school, because of his weight problem, and
because of his dad's cancer. Imagine me walking into that Aikido
studio, dreaming of becoming the next Bruce Lee. Yeah, it's probably true: When I walked in there, I wanted to hit something, to hit
somebody.

But what did I end up doing instead? Sitting there in the dojo and
learning about ... breathing. Yes, breathing.

Sensei took me under his wing and began teaching the importance
of what Aikido refers to as "Ki breathing," which is literally an exer-

cise in, well, breathing. But it's not just regular breathing, of course. It is breathing with a purpose. When we practice Ki breathing, we try to focus entirely on our "hara," or "one point," the spot just beneath our belly buttons that serves as our spiritual and emotional "center." We inhale deeply, exhale deeply, and imagine our breath pulled out of us, ever so slowly, like a string.

The idea is to get ourselves thinking about one thing and one thing only — our breathing — as a means of clearing away all of the clutter in our heads. Ki breathing, at its best, can wipe away from our brains all of the worries of the day and allow us, for just a short while, to exist in peace, clarity, and calmness. Ki breathing re-energizes us and relaxes us. It frees us from stress. It brings us back to center.

It is a wonderful thing. It really is. But like I said, *it's not easy.*

I have been practicing Aikido now for more than two decades, and as a result I've spent countless hours practicing my breathing. Yet, I find that it's still extremely difficult to achieve true relaxation, true calmness, and true peace.

I was a worried, anxious kid and, at times, I'm a worried, anxious adult. I still have trouble sleeping at night — my head hits the pillow, my mind starts racing, and the next thing you know, my heart is racing, too. There's only one thing I can do when that happens: Close my eyes, focus on my hara, breathe deeply, and try, once again, to wipe away the worry.

When I pull this off, I sleep much better. And wake up much happier, too.

Look, the reality is this: Neither you nor I are ever going to completely free ourselves from worry.

We're never going to completely rid ourselves of stress. We're never going to be able to live our lives in a continual state of peace and calm, of relaxation, focus, and happiness. But, that peace, that calmness, is still worth striving for.

And again, to find that peace and calmness, you don't need to be a yoga master locked away in your personal dojo or laying out in some beautiful grassy field with the stars all around you. You can achieve — and must achieve — glimpses of calmness no matter where you are, or what you're doing. You can achieve relaxation and calmness even at the most stressful of times.

If you're preparing for a big presentation, of course you're going to be nervous. Your palms will get sweaty, your mouth will get dry, and your heart will begin to race. But the moment that happens — the moment you feel yourself become overwhelmed — take a step back and just *check out*.

Practice your breathing. Focus on the good in your life. Clear your head of the clutter. Then open your eyes and do your work. Believe me: A relaxed you will be more persuasive, more powerful, and more successful.

If you're about to close a big business deal, of course you're going to be tense, you're going to fret about every last deal of the contract, and your stress levels are going to be soaring. But you can't walk into that room in a tizzy, wrapped up in worry and doubt. So, before you close the deal, *check out*. Practice your breathing. Find your focus. Then go get the deal done.

There have been many times in my career as a magician when I've been terrified before heading out on stage. One particular event stands out for me. It was a really big one in which I was given the absolute worst slot on the agenda — just after lunch and just before the day's headliner. I remember people coming up to me and saying, "Tough break, Todd." As if I needed them to tell me that.

I knew exactly what I was getting into: The audience was going to be sleepy. They were going to be anxious to see the *next* speaker. And since they didn't know who in the hell I was, they probably weren't going to be all that interested in what I had to say, either.

If I was going to succeed, I was going to have to hit them hard — right off the bat. I knew if they picked up on any insecurity, any nervousness, or any stress, it would be a disaster. It was absolutely essential that I take the stage in a state of complete relaxation, calmness, peace, and confidence.

That's what I did — and by all accounts, I killed that day.

So, yes, relaxation and calmness can make you better at your job. They can make you a better manager, and they can make you a better leader, too.

But let's not forget, ultimately, what this book is about. This book is about living a better, happier, healthier, and more balanced *life*.

And, *if* you can find relaxation every day, and if you can maintain a sense of calm with the world churning all around, you will have a better, happier, healthier, and more balanced life.

These are hard times in our country and the entire world. When Wall Street collapsed back in 2008, life changed — for the worse — for a lot of us. Some of us lost our life savings, some lost our homes, some lost our jobs, and some have never gotten those jobs back.

I'm not naïve enough to believe that Ki breathing, meditation, or going out with your buddies for a beer and some laughs (and yes, that's relaxation, too), can completely take away the pain or the worry of this difficult time. But I do believe that these things — things that can help us attain some level of relaxation and calmness — can make a difference.

It's as simple as this: We cannot live happily if we cannot relax. We cannot appreciate the beauty of this world if we cannot be calm.

We all dream of "world peace," and, yes, that would be a wonderful thing. But we, as individuals, cannot make such a massive, overwhelming, impossible dream come true on our own. All we can do is make our world more peaceful, more calm, and more beautiful. In other words, more balanced.

As I've said before, I struggle with relaxation, too. And when the kids are screaming and my BlackBerry is blowing up, it's hard for me to find any sense of calm. I am human, after all, and as imperfect as anyone else.

But I also can say that my life has been made all the more happy — and so have the lives of my friends and family — simply because I've made it a goal to find relaxation and calmness. I strive for both every day.

For me, that striving comes in the form of Ki breathing — those precious moments when I can simply exist, without the weight of the world on my shoulders. For you, that striving may come in a different form.

Maybe you will find your relaxation and calmness in the garden. Maybe, like my mother, you will find it in the kitchen, baking bread for your family. Maybe you will find it in music. Maybe you will find it in the darkness and quiet of your bedroom, in those reflective moments just before you drift away to sleep. Or, maybe you will find it someplace that I cannot even fathom.

But, I'm telling you, *you must find it.*

Do not let life run you down. Do not give in to stress and worry. You must be able to relax and appreciate the simple beauty of life. You must be able to remain calm in the face of life's troubles — to understand that most of those troubles are not really troubles at all. You must try every day to achieve both of these things.

If you can, you will be a better person, a happier person, and a more balanced person.

CHAPTER 4

The Key to a Balanced Diet? Common Sense

I spent four years of my life studying the science of nutrition. Then, I spent several more years plying my trade in a hospital, using what I learned in college, to make sure the patients were eating the healthiest, most nutritious foods possible. It was a job I enjoyed, and one I took very seriously — because I take nutrition very seriously.

I could probably spend the next five chapters of this book regurgitating all of the information I learned in college about nutrition. I could quote from papers written by some of the smartest people in the field. I could talk about calories and fat calories, LDL cholesterol and HDL cholesterol, and vitamins and nutrients. I could talk about all of the knowledge that goes into designing a well-balanced meal. There's a lot of science behind nutrition, a lot of research, and it can be a complicated field.

But you know what? That would probably bore you.

I'm not going to bother you with any of that stuff. I'm not going to dwell on research papers or bog our discussion down with too many details.

As much as I respect the field of nutrition, and as much as I admire the researchers who work so diligently to turn up new and important information about nutrition, I believe that a healthy, balanced diet can be achieved very, very simply.

You know what you need to build a healthy diet for yourself? Basic common sense. That's it.

Now, I know that can be hard to believe. You're probably thinking:

"Nope. There's a lot more to it than that." And you know what? I completely understand why you might feel that way. The diet industry today is a multibillion dollar behemoth, and it's growing larger each and every day. In a way, it's an industry designed to intentionally make losing weight and eating well seem a lot more complicated than it actually is. And it does a great job of confusing a lot of people. Oh, and it makes a whole lot of money, too.

Just think for a moment about all the different companies that are reaping huge profits by simply promising to help people lose a few pounds. We have Jenny Craig, WeightWatchers, Nutrisystem, and Slim-Fast, among others. We have gyms on every corner and health food stores on every other corner. We flock to exercise classes and buy into the latest dieting fads — the South Beach Diet, the Malibu diet, the Atkins diet.

In short, we are a nation *starved* for health — and frustrated by our fat.

We all want to be skinnier. We all want to feel better, and live better, and look better. And we're so darn desperate for healthy living — so desperate to make ourselves better, skinner, and happier — that we're willing to pay almost any price for it. Just imagine how much money we as a nation would be willing to pay for a proven, effective, and safe weight-loss pill. $10 per pill? $20 per pill? Maybe $100 per pill?

Here's the bad news: No such pill exists. And I don't expect one to be coming down the pike anytime soon, either. Which means ... you're on your own. If you want to lose weight, if you want to look better at the beach, if you just want to feel more comfortable in your own skin, you're going to have to do it on your own. Sorry.

But, here's the good news: Just like I said at the start of this chapter, *losing weight is not that difficult.* Eating healthy is not that difficult. Nutrition is not that difficult.

In fact, I am willing to bet that you already know everything you need to know to make your diet healthy, balanced, and nutritious. You've probably known everything you need to know to do this stuff for years now. Your parents knew it. Your grandparents knew. Everyone knows it.

At the end of the day, this whole nutrition thing is basic common sense.

Don't believe me? Well, read on.

Do me a favor.

Take a peek, right now, inside your pantry, or your refrigerator, or wherever it is you keep your food. I want you to take a good look at what you've got in there, and make a quick mental inventory of your food situation.

Now, I want you to answer a question: How much of that food is, you know, *real food*? And no, this is not a difficult question to answer. I am quite certain you know very well what I mean by "real food."

Real foods are fruit, vegetables, and grains. Real foods are milk, eggs, cheese, and yogurt. That big bowl of leftover pasta? Yeah, that's real food. So are those leftover grilled chicken breasts, those slices of pizza, even those pork chops.

Some of those foods certainly have their faults. But at the end of the day, at least you know it's real food — because you know what they're made of. Grilled chicken, you can be certain, is actually chicken. The pizza? It's bread and tomato sauce and cheese. And the pork chops? Well, they're pork chops.

Should you eat pork every night? No, probably not. But as a dietitian, well, I wouldn't get upset if you ate pork chops every once in a while.

But I'm sure you're wondering what does get me upset?

Well, how about that two-liter jug of soda there on the fridge door? Or, the package of Twinkies in the pantry? Or that bag of "cheese puffs"? Or the multi-colored "breakfast cereal" that is made almost entirely of sugar and food coloring? And don't think I didn't notice the bag of day-old fast-food leftovers, either.

All of that stuff — the processed *fake foods* that you've got hiding in that pantry — is the kind of stuff that makes me upset. Really upset.

And here's why: Because that stuff is garbage. Complete garbage. It's not real food. In fact, it's barely food at all. Your first step toward a healthy, balanced diet, then, is to toss the trash into the trash.

Out with the Twinkies and cheese puffs. Out with the soda. Out with that horrible sugar cereal. And out with the fast food.

Say goodbye to all of it — and promise me you'll never eat it again.

Again, I have to point out that there's nothing good in *any* of that stuff. It's terrible, unhealthy food that will make you miserable.

Of course, you didn't need me to tell you that. You know very well just how horribly unhealthy those alleged "foods" are.

You know it by your waistline, which has steadily expanded since you began eating that stuff (no coincidence, by the way). You also know it by the way those "foods" make you feel. Be honest, now: How do you feel about five minutes after you wolf down a Big Mac?

Bloated? Achy? Sick? Yeah, that's what I thought.

The reason, of course, is simple: Those Twinkies and cheese puffs and soda and fast food garbage are nothing more than low-grade poison dressed up as food.

The human body can endure plenty, and our species has ingested a lot of odd stuff over the years. But, I am rather certain that we were never intended to eat Twinkies. Maybe someday that will change. Maybe someday we'll evolve enough to eat Twinkies without issue. But we're not there yet.

The numbers speak for themselves.

According to some estimates, more than 60 percent of all American children are obese. Not just overweight. Not just a little chunky. *Obese.*

In case you were wondering, that means they are *morbidly overweight.* Oh, and this is not just about teenagers, either. Because believe it or not, those same studies also tell us that more than 20 percent of our preschoolers — preschoolers! — are obese, too.

Maybe those numbers shock you. But, if you really think about it, should you be shocked? Should you even be surprised? I mean, take a look around you. Look at the people you interact with every single day. How many of those people could you say are actually healthy? How many are flat-out unhealthy? Unfortunately, probably most of them.

As a nation, we are just way too fat. In fact, we are the unhealthiest, fattest nation in the history of the world. And it doesn't appear that this is going to change anytime soon.

We are just getting fatter, and fatter, and fatter.

And what about those bad habits our grandparents passed down to our parents? Well, our parents passed them down to us. Now, we're passing them down to our children — and they very well could end up passing them down to their children, too. Because we seem so unwilling to change our habits, our kids — and our kids' kids — are going to pay the price for the rest of their lives. They will battle cancer and heart disease, diabetes, and arthritis. They'll battle depression, too. Because we all know, when we aren't physically healthy, we can't be mentally healthy, either.

It's sad but true: We are trapped in a vicious, destructive cycle of poor nutrition and unbalanced living.

However, you *don't* have to let that cycle destroy your family. You don't have to live unhappily and eat unhealthily, and you don't have to let your kids do so, either.

Because no matter how you've been living up until now, and no matter what you've been eating up until now, you can make the decision — right now — to live better and eat better from here on out.

It's not that hard to do.

Here's something most dietitians may not admit, but I will: I like going out for beers with my buddies. Oh, I enjoy a good cheeseburger, too. In fact, I love a cheeseburger. Who doesn't?

We are put on this Earth to live well, and part of living well is treating ourselves to something a little bit decadent now and again. So yeah, go ahead. Have a couple beers during the big game. Enjoy that big old steak dinner. Order the cheesecake for dessert.

And then the next day, make sure you get your exercise in. *And don't have another big old steak.*

Is that so hard? No, I didn't think so.

But this is exactly the kind of basic, simple behavior — a common-sense decision to not overindulge two days in a row — that can keep you on the path toward a healthy life, not to mention a relatively slim waistline. This is exactly the kind of behavior that, if incorporated into your daily decision-making, will bring you a sense of real nutritional balance.

When it comes to diet, I don't have any hard and fast rules for you. I don't have a list of "forbidden foods." And I certainly don't have a magic bullet method for helping you lose 20 pounds.

What I do have are six simple principles — broad, basic, easy-to-understand principles — that I believe can keep you, and your family, feeling good and looking good for generations to come.

Those principles are as follows:

Enjoy everything in moderation. This one speaks for itself. Like I said earlier, I love grabbing a couple beers with the guys. Heck, I believe you need to grab a couple beers with the guys every once in a while. But you should not grab a couple beers with the guys every night. You should not go out for hot wings every night. You should not eat ice cream every night. This is plain old common sense. And I don't think this is a particularly difficult rule to follow, either. If you want to feel healthy, if you want to be healthy, you just can't overindulge.

Exercise regularly. We are going to address physical fitness in the next chapter, but a healthy diet won't do you much good if you don't put your body to the test now and again. Regular exercise is absolutely essential. Work up a sweat at least five times each week.

Limit or completely avoid processed foods. This is a big one for me, which is why the first part of this chapter harps on it so much. Let me emphasize it again, though, because it's just so important: Super-processed foods are death in a bag. This stuff is not food. You simply shouldn't be eating it. Your kids shouldn't be eating it, either. Don't give them that garbage. Because if you give it to them, they'll start to believe that it's worthwhile — that it has value. They will accept those foods as part of a healthy diet. You can't let them think that. Do your kids a favor. When you feed them, feed them real food.

Be a nutritional role model for your children. Your kids will follow your lead. Believe me, they will. So eat healthy, and be healthy. If you're healthy, chances are they'll be healthy, too.

Stick with whole-grain foods. Look, I know most of us grew up on Wonder bread and white rice. And I know that our parents' generation probably thinks we're crazy for making such a big deal about whole-grain breads. I mean, to them, bread is bread. Wheat bread, white bread — what's the difference, right? Wrong. The facts and science are clear: Whole-grain breads and whole-grain foods, in general, are much healthier than that old-school white bread. These breads contain vitamins, minerals, and essential fatty acids that white bread simply doesn't. Some studies also show that whole-grain breads help make you feel fuller longer, too.

Enjoy food. This might be the most important point of all. I want you to love food. I want you to teach your children to love food. I want you to cook with your kids. I want you to try new things — and encourage your kids to try new things. Food is one of the great pleasures in life. So, for goodness sake, enjoy it. Savor it.

Follow these principles and I promise you, you will be well on your way to achieving a more balanced diet — and a more balanced life.

CHAPTER 5

Making 'The Choice': How to Overcome Inertia and Stay Physically Fit

If you've read this far, then you probably realize I'm a pretty busy guy.

In fact, around the time I was writing this book, I was juggling not one, but *two* jobs — my "day job" as a pharmaceutical salesman, and a budding career in magic — as well as all of my responsibilities as a family man, not to mention all of that other stuff that makes life these days oh-so-complicated. More days than not, I am tied up with something or other — phone calls, sales calls, magic shows, paperwork, kids' activities — from the moment I wake up until the moment I go to bed. And even when I go to bed, the day isn't really over; our kids aren't the greatest sleepers.

But you know what? This kind of life — this crazy, always-on-the-go life — hardly makes me unique. Because I'm fairly certain *my* crazy life mirrors *your* crazy life. And your friends' crazy lives. And your neighbors' crazy lives. And the crazy lives of just about everyone else these days, too.

It doesn't take a genius to see that Americans are living busier and more hectic lives than any people in any country have ever lived before.

We work hard — and though we don't play near enough, we play hard, too. We expect everyone else to work just as hard as us. We even make our kids work hard. We are on the go, endlessly.

It's insanity. It really is.

And yet, it is our reality. So, we have to live with it.

And the sad truth is that our nation is not suddenly going to adopt a less-busy lifestyle. Corporations are not going to band together and, out of the goodness of their hearts, suddenly adopt a four-day workweek. Banks are not going to forgive our debts or lower the principal on our mortgages. Our culture is not going to suddenly expect us to do less. If anything, we're headed in the opposite direction — more work, more debt, and more stress.

And this translates into less time to look after ourselves. Less time to relax. Less time to meditate. Less time to exercise.

Yes, exercise. Remember exercise?

I don't consider myself a judgmental person. And, as I've said before and will say again: I have my faults. Many of them, actually.

And having been "the fat kid" myself, I know how easy it can be to slip into bad habits, and how easy it can be to allow those habits to become, well, routine. I know how hard it can be, when you're down and depressed and feeling lazy, to get up off the couch and go for a run. I know how it feels to wake up one day, look in the mirror and wonder, "How did I end up like this?" I also know that being a fat person doesn't mean you're a bad person.

I've been overweight before and may be overweight again; it's certainly not impossible. Then again, I don't think it's likely. I would even dare say it's very unlikely.

And there's one reason why: I exercise.

Maybe it would be more accurate to say I make time for exercise in my life. You could probably say I'm fanatical about it.

Yes, I'm very, very busy. And, yes, there are a lot of nights, in those blissfully peaceful moments after we put the kids to bed, when there is nothing I'd rather do than crash out on the couch, grab a beer, and turn myself into a vegetable. On a few select nights, I let myself do just that (no, I didn't forget that big chapter about "Relaxation.")

Most nights, however, I don't crash out. I don't grab a beer. I don't collapse on the couch. I don't spend two hours vegging out in front of the television. Because most nights, even when I'm exhausted and totally not in the mood, I make myself do the one thing that was most responsible for helping me lose all that weight back in my high school days, and the one thing that will prevent me from gaining 100 pounds in the future: I exercise.

I make the *choice* to exercise. You can make the same choice, too.

If you're already making that choice, I commend you. And if you're not, I just have one question: *Why not?*

I bet I know what your answer was to that last question.

I bet you said this: "I'm too busy. I don't have time to exercise. If I didn't work so much, if I didn't have the kids, sure, I'd exercise. But my life is too crazy. There's just no time to work out. Maybe in a couple years I can get back into it. But now? No, not now. Just too busy."

Yeah, fine.

You know what I say to all of that? Hogwash. Baloney. To put it more bluntly: *That's B.S.*

Offended? Well, sorry. I'm just not buying it. And, please, don't even waste your breath trying to make the case that *your* life is so uniquely busy that you literally "do not have the time" to exercise. Don't try to tell me that you, unlike everyone else in this world, are the sole person who cannot carve 30 minutes out of your day to engage in an activity that will not only keep you slimmer and more fit, but also make you a happier, healthier, and generally more balanced person. Do not try to sell me on the idea that *you* are any less busy than *I* am. Because I assure you, I'm really busy. Really, really busy.

You know who else is really, really busy? The president of the United States.

Yes, I'm talking about President Barack Obama. The most powerful man in the world. The man who is charged with leading the wealthiest society in world history. The man who, as I write this, is attempting to sway world opinion on global warming and push through the most radical health care reform package in decades, while at the same time overseeing our nation's ongoing involvement in Iraq, directing the escalation of the war in Afghanistan, and dealing with who-knows-how-many other national security threats. Just imagine carrying his BlackBerry for a day.

President Obama — like all of the presidents before him — wakes up every day with the world literally on his shoulders, and pressures that you and I cannot even begin to fathom. There is not a single issue that his nation faces that he is not responsible for handling.

His each and every day is a parade of meetings and public appear-
ances and politicking and traveling. Heck, the man is so darned busy
that his daily calendar is detailed *to the minute*; while you and I have
meetings that start at 10 a.m., President Obama has meetings that
start at 10:07 a.m. Not a single minute is wasted.

Oh, and he's got a family, too — a wife and two young girls. The
man may be President, but he's still a father. We all know how hectic
that can be.

But here's the thing: President Obama makes time *almost every
day* to exercise.

I mean, take a look at the guy. He's in great shape — one might
even say outstanding shape — which is a darn near miracle for a
guy in a position like his (a position that would drive many a man
to drink too much, eat too much, and spend too much time behind a
desk, rather than on a treadmill).

President Obama, though, hasn't let his job — or the massive
responsibilities that job brings — get in the way of what must always
be his No. 1 priority: taking care of himself.

What President Obama understands is the very thing that I'm
going to spend the rest of this chapter trying to drill into your head,
too: Making the choice to exercise is as fundamental to a healthy,
balanced, and successful life as making the choice to do well at your
job, making the choice to be good to your kids, or making the choice
to make sound financial decisions.

When you make the choice to exercise — and this is a choice you
must make, almost every day — you are essentially making a statement about what you value, about the kind of person you want to be,
and about the kind of life you want to live. By making the choice to
exercise, you are telling the world: you care about your health; you
want to be there to take care of your children — and your children's
children; you are the kind of person who wants to enjoy *everything*
life has to offer; and you're also the kind of person who is willing to
make the sacrifices required to make that happen.

So, what kind of person do you want to be? What do *you* want
out of life? How do you want to be perceived? Do you want success?
Do you want happiness? Do you want balance?

Yes? Well, great.

Then get on that treadmill. Go for a run. Sign up for a fitness class. Start going to yoga. Take up Aikido (speaking from experience, I can assure you, it works). Buy a bike — and ride it. Heck, just get up off your butt and take a nice long walk. That counts, too. I promise.

Do any of those things. *Any* of them. Just be sure you get that heart rate up. Break a sweat. Push yourself a little. And then — well, then do it again tomorrow, and the next day, and the next day ... forever.

Because here's the secret: It's not really about what kind of exercise you do. It's more or less about making commonsense, health-conscious decisions, each and every day. Just like your diet, it's about consistency. It's about repetition. It's about discipline. *That's* what brings you a healthy lifestyle.

It's not the choice you make *today* that matters, rather than the choice you make tomorrow. It certainly sounds nice to boldly proclaim, "I will work out every day for the rest of my life!" But, what does that really mean. What matters is not the promise you make to yourself. What matters is keeping that promise.

And, no, it's not always easy.

But you've got to do it anyway. If you want to lose weight, if you want to feel better about yourself, if you want to have a happier life, well, you are going to have to work for it. You're going to have to work really, really hard for it. Sorry, that's just the way it is.

I know you probably know this already, but let me assure you once more of the following truth: *There is no easy way to stay in shape.*

There is no magical made-for-TV product that will shrink your waistline. There is no weight-loss pill. There is no miracle cure.

There is just hard work, dedication, and plain old-fashioned *willpower*. There is just that choice — that one choice you and I and everybody else has to make every single day.

So here's the question: Will you make the right choice?

If you're not ready to answer "yes," then you might as well stop reading now. There's no point in your continuing. Because believe me, if you're not willing to exercise, you're never going to achieve balance, and you might as well just head back to the couch.

But, if you *are* ready to answer, "yes," well, congratulations! You've made the right choice. Now all you have to do is go exercise.

Right now.

Yes, put down the book. Put it down.

Get up out of your chair. Go to your room. Change into your workout clothes and, please, just go do something. Give me 50 pushups. Go for a run. Do some yoga. Hop on the stationary bike. Do something. I don't care what time it is. I want you to go exercise *now*.

And here's why: There's never going to be a "convenient" time to work out. There just isn't. There will always be an excuse for why you *can't* work out. And most everyone else in America seems as though they're fairly adept at using those excuses.

Don't let yourself fall into that trap. Don't give yourself an easy out. Make yourself exercise even when you don't feel like exercising. Make yourself work out even when working out seems like the least sensible thing you can do.

Like, for instance, right now.

I'm serious: Right now.

Go ahead. I'm not going anywhere. I'll see you when you get back.

See you in 30 minutes.

Have a good workout.

Now that felt good, right?

Maybe it wasn't "easy," but I bet it sure was invigorating — more invigorating than watching TV at least.

Don't you feel energized? Happier? Alive?

Don't you just feel a whole lot better than you did 30 minutes ago?

Yep, that's what I thought.

And here's the good news: That feeling is there for the taking. Every single day.

All you have to do, of course, is make the choice to grab it. All you have to do is make your mind beat your body. All you have to do is get yourself out of that funk, and out of that recliner, and — voila — just 30 minutes later you'll be feeling a whole lot better about yourself — guaranteed.

It all sounds so easy, right? So *simple*. And it is that simple, but at the same time it's also hard. See, I have been doing Aikido for about 20 years now. That means I've been heading down to the dojo for about 20 years now, too.

And do you know what the single biggest lesson I've learned about exercise in all of that time is? The hardest part about exercise is not the exercise itself. Nope. The hardest part about exercise is getting yourself to just *start doing the exercise.*

It's a simple matter of inertia. Think about it: When you're crashed out on your couch, it's a lot easier to stay crashed out on our couch than it is to go to the gym, or the dojo, or even the treadmill in your basement. I know this as much as anyone; it's as hard for me to get myself to the dojo as it is for you to get down to the gym.

I know this stuff is not easy. But, you know what? I don't care.

I've experienced life as a sloth and, believe me, it's not fun. It's borderline miserable, actually. Being fat makes you self-conscious. It makes you sluggish. It makes you unhappy and uninspired. It affects your ability to make friends. It affects your ability to do business.

All of that weight can literally weigh down your entire life. It's like living life with a wet blanket wrapped around you — a wet blanket of bad health and depression. When you're fat and out of shape, you look miserable, you feel miserable, and you are miserable.

But living healthy? Well, I don't know how else to say it: It's just a whole lot more fun to be alive when you're proud of what you are. It's a lot more fun to be alive when you feel healthy, not sick. It's a lot more fun to be alive when you can wake up in the morning, look yourself in the mirror, and say, "Not bad. Not bad at all."

Once you achieve that feeling, I promise you, you're not going to want to give it up.

So, to start, you've got to overcome that inertia. You have to get up off of that couch, and you have to break a sweat. And, you have to keep doing it from here on out.

I won't tell you it will always be easy. I won't tell you that it will always be fun. I'll only tell you that *it will make a difference.* It will make you happier. It will make you skinnier. It will make you more confident, more poised, and less stressed.

It will, above all else, make you more balanced.

CHAPTER 6

Your Mother Was Right — Posture Matters

I am here to tell you that posture — *good* posture, specifically — matters. It really does.

In fact, good posture is every bit as essential to healthy, happy, and successful living as a good diet, a positive outlook, and a regular exercise regimen. Good posture can make a difference — a huge difference — in how you feel about yourself, and how others feel about you. Good posture is an absolutely essential element of The Balance Diet.

You cannot achieve true balance — and, by extension, true health and true happiness — without it.

Maybe you've gone along with everything I've said in this book so far, and bought into my argument that *balanced* living is the key to *good* living. Maybe you've already taken steps to improve your diet. Maybe you've already joined the gym or taken up running or signed up for martial arts classes. Maybe you're making a little bit of time each day for meditation. Maybe you've taken on the challenge of trying to achieve a sense of calm. And maybe all of those efforts have already paid dividends for you.

But maybe you're looking at boring old posture — the good old-fashioned habit of just standing up straight — as a somewhat less important element of this book, a somewhat less compelling aspect of this little philosophy that I call The Balance Diet. And so, maybe, you're thinking that you'll just skip ahead to the next chapter and worry about this posture business later.

I can understand that, because even I'll admit that posture isn't the most glamorous of topics.

Posture is something your mother nagged you about when you were a kid. It's something those strict nuns in Catholic school harped about day in and day out. It's something your doctor mentions most every time you see him. It's something that you — and many other people, unfortunately — just don't seem to care about, take all that seriously, or even think about.

For far too many people, posture is, well, *irrelevant*. They believe the way they stand is the way they stand, and the way they sit is the way they sit. There's no more point to changing their posture, they reason, than there is to change the way they walk or the color of their hair. Their posture — either good or bad — is something beyond their control. They can't decide how tall they are, they can't decide what color their eyes are, and they can't control how straight — or crooked — their backs are. Their posture is their posture, for good or ill. They've just got to live with it.

Right? Wrong.

Not only *can* we control our posture, but we *must* control our posture — not just to make our mothers happy, no. Not just to get the nuns off our backs and not just because the doctor tells us to.

But rather, we should do it for the very sake of our health and the very sake of our careers.

Yes, our careers.

I'll get into the health benefits of good posture in just a bit. But first, I want to talk a bit about how good posture can impact us socially, professionally — and financially.

Here's an example that proves my point.

With the events that occurred on September 11, 2001, the twin towers of the World Trade Center lay in ruins, as did much of the Pentagon and a doomed airliner in the Pennsylvania countryside. Thousands of Americans had just been murdered, in New York, Washington, and Western Pennsylvania, in the single worst terrorist attack in the history of the modern world.

Our nation was reeling. Shocked. Terrified. And, maybe more than anything else, looking for leadership. Begging to be *led*.

So, President George W. Bush headed up to lower Manhattan, where he visited Ground Zero to rally the poor rescue workers faced with the daunting task of trying to find survivors. The President, decked out in blue jeans and a work shirt, took a megaphone and began to address the men and women standing down below.

However, his megaphone wasn't quite loud enough. "We can't hear you!" bellowed one worker.

"Well, I can hear you," President Bush responded. "I hear you. The rest of the world hears you. And the people who knocked these buildings down will hear from all of us soon."

The crowd roared at what they had just seen. This was no planned speech. This was no Madison Avenue moment. Rather, it was President Bush speaking from the heart.

You see, let's go back to President Bush for a moment.

As I said at the start of this chapter, that scene at Ground Zero was powerful for two reasons. First, because of *what* the President said. Second, because of *how* he said it. And yes, those are two different things.

Here's why: At a time when the mighty United States was down and out — at a time when this great nation was a figurative dog with its tail between its legs — our President was talking boldly and standing tall.

And you know what? We believed him. We believed him because when President Bush uttered those words, he was standing straight, tall, and powerful.

The crowd there at Ground Zero roared its approval not just because they liked what the President said; they roared their approval because they believed what he said. And, they *believed* what he said, in part, because of his *posture*.

The reality is this: The people in this world who are most successful are those who have good posture; the people in this world who demand the most respect are those who walk straight and tall; the people in this world who we look to for leadership are those who are confident enough to carry themselves with strength, dignity, and forthrightness. Simply put, the people who make it in this world have great posture.

President Bush had great posture then, and President Obama has it today.

Martin Luther King, Jr. had great posture.

Muhammad Ali, Michael Jordan, Joe Montana, and all of the

sports stars of yesteryear had great posture. Additionally, all of the great sports stars of today have great posture, too, such as Peyton Manning, LeBron James, and Derek Jeter, among others.

By rule and by practice, these men are not *slouches*. By the very way they carry themselves, they announce to the world that they are leaders.

But here's the thing: It's not just the rich and famous, the powerful and super-successful, that can demand respect, or convey a sense of authority, through great posture. It's you and me, too. The power of good posture is available to all of us.

Believe me, I *know* this to be true.

Sensei first taught me about the value of good posture back in the Northeast Philadelphia dojo. In the 20 years since, I've seen first-hand how practicing good posture — simply being aware of it, and making sure it is correct — can impact how we experience the world, how we feel about the world, and how the world feels about us.

Good posture affects our personal relationships. It affects our social standing. It impacts our *financial bottom line*.

Really, it does.

For much of my adult life, I've made my living as a salesman, and my success or failure doesn't have nearly as much to do with *what* I'm selling as it does *how* I go about selling it.

When I am seeing a potential new client, I know the first impression means *absolutely everything*. When I walk in that door, the person waiting inside is going to make a snap judgment — either consciously or subconsciously — about whether they like and/or respect me. My sale won't be made in the 15 minutes I spend pitching my product, but rather in the 15 *seconds* I spend entering that room and establishing my presence.

So, you can be darn sure that each and every time I confront those 15 seconds — the 15 seconds that make me or break me — I am sure to enter the room with authority, and spectacular posture.

And you know what? It's worked out pretty nicely for me. I'm not saying *all* of my sales success can be attributed to my posture. But I am saying my posture has made a difference. A huge difference in my opinion.

Think I'm making too much of this posture stuff? Well, I'm not.

When I wrote about nutrition and exercise in previous chapters, there were two words that I found myself using over and over again: common sense.

I concluded that creating a healthy diet for yourself comes down to plain old common sense. And crafting an effective fitness plan? Well, that's about common sense, too. There's no mystery to any of it. The facts are clear. We know what's good for us. We know what's bad for us. The only trick is making the right choices.

It's the same deal with posture. Good posture is just *good for you.* There's no disputing it. So, for goodness sake, start paying attention to it!

Imagine for a moment that you are walking down an empty city street, late at night, and you are being approached by a large group of young men. You don't know if they're good or bad kids. You don't know if they mean ill or well. All you know is that you're walking toward them, they're walking toward you, and, eventually, your paths are going to cross. You are going to have to confront that group, whether you like it or not.

So here are your choices: You can either walk toward them looking scared — shoulders slouched, eyes averted, and head down — or you can walk toward them looking unfazed — upright posture, eyes ahead, head up, and walking tall.

It's a no-brainer, right? I mean, why would you ever choose the former? Why would you choose to look vulnerable? Why would you *invite* an attack?

It goes right back to the whole common sense thing, guys. I admit this particular example may be an extreme one. But, it is an illustrative one, too, because it shows so very clearly the stark contrast in the messages sent by bad posture ("I am weak") and good posture ("Attack me if you must, but you're in for a fight").

Yes, posture can say that much. It really can. And not just on an abandoned city street, either. Good posture can communicate your very worth, each and every day. It is, I believe, the most powerful non-verbal communication we can make.

Walking with good posture tells the world: "I am worthy of your respect." It tells the world: "I believe in myself, and so you should believe in me, too." And, it tells the world: "Hire me. Buy from me.

Work with me. Because I am good at what I do, and I am a person to be reckoned with."

Good posture shapes the way people look at us, and can ultimately make the difference between a successful life and a lifelong struggle.

But you know what else posture can do? It can flat-out make us healthier.

According to health professionals, the benefits of good posture include everything from reduced risk of back pain and back injury to better muscle and organ function. Doctors go on to say that good posture can make us more energetic, more focused, less stressed, and better able to concentrate on the tasks that await us every single day. Good posture makes us look and feel taller. It makes us more confident. It can even make us look younger. In essence, good posture is the key to unlocking all of our physical ability. In other words, without good posture, we can never achieve our optimum level of fitness.

Medicine has come a long way in recent decades, and as more and more doctors embrace the ideas behind holistic medicine — which, by the way, are really quite similar to the ideas that the Japanese martial arts have been preaching for centuries — they are more and more willing to look at the human body not as a collection of individual pieces and parts, but rather a complete *system*.

Holding that system together, of course, is our spinal column — our physical and neurological power base. All of our powers — both physical and mental — are connected in some way to our backs. So it's a no-brainer: We need to take care of them.

And here's the good news: Doing so is very, very easy.

In fact, you can start right now by sitting up straight; by walking tall; by being fully aware, at all times, of how you are carrying yourself; and by making a mental note, each and every morning, to live the day ahead with good, strong, confident, and healthy posture.

In Aikido, we tell ourselves that we must have good posture in everything we do. Which is why we exercise good posture at the dojo, why we exercise good posture during our drive to the dojo, and why we exercise good posture on the way home from the dojo.

We exercise good posture at home, at work, and while meditating. Really, we practice it while doing anything and everything.

We understand, just as George W. Bush understood, that our posture does matter. So, we make sure that the practice of good posture is as central to our daily healthy lives as good nutrition, a strong exercise program, a commitment to calmness and relaxation, and, of course, our ongoing pursuit of a balanced life.

CHAPTER 7

Finding the Magic in Your Life

Where's the magic in this world?

Well, take a look around you. Take a look at this world. Take a look at your *life*. Look at your kids. Look at your wife. Take a peek out your window. Take in the flowers. The trees. That stunningly clear blue sky. The Sun and the Moon and the uncountable stars.

Think about the absolute miracle of childbirth — and then realize that this miracle happens millions of times, every day. Appreciate, if you even can, the raw power of Niagara Falls. The impossible enormity of the Grand Canyon. The vastness of the oceans. The otherworldliness of Mt. Everest — and the incredible among us who have actually climbed it (and lived to tell the tale).

Most of all, reflect about all of the little things you see and do every day, but never really appreciate — not enough, at least: the sunrise and the sunset; the laughter of your children; good times with good friends; delicious food; and wonderful wine.

Think about the endless possibility that awaits you every morning, and the peaceful moments of reflection that are there for the taking every evening.

After thinking about all of that, just try to tell me you don't believe there is any magic in this world. Just try to tell me this life isn't full of mysteries and miracles, large and small. Just try to tell me that we shouldn't wake up every day with a sense of absolute wonderment at what is all around us. Just try to tell me I shouldn't believe in magic.

The title of this book is *The Magic of Balanced Living*, after all, and you're probably figuring that magic itself is central to this little philosophy I call The Balance Diet. Well, you'd be right about that.

Yes, I do believe in magic — just not in the way you're probably thinking.

I guess the best way to say it is this: It's not that I necessarily believe in magic itself, but rather that I believe in the *power* of magic.

I know that discovering magic, and understanding magic, has helped me better understand my life. Which is why I believe magic can also help you navigate life's ups and downs, better appreciate the blessings you've been given, and, of course, live a more balanced life. I believe magic can teach us about our lives — and help us live our lives better.

The bottom line? Simple: Magic is just as essential to The Balance Diet as exercise and nutrition, and just as important to balanced living as a positive mind and a sense of calm.

Magic can be transformative. It can ease our pain. It can bring color to our lives.

But magic can't do any of that if we choose to ignore it. If we can't, or won't, accept that there's magic in this world, then magic won't find us, and our lives will be a little less full as a result.

I discovered magic by accident.

Which, in itself, is somewhat magical when you think about it. I had gone about 30 years without even thinking twice about magic. Then one day, I met a guy who just happened to be a magician. He showed me a card trick, and I was hooked.

Magic arrived in my life suddenly and unexpectedly; its impact was immediate and profound. And, just like that, my life was changed. My magic career wasn't possible before that day. Heck, this book wasn't possible before that day. And yes, there's an obvious lesson here: Don't look at any day as "just another day," because there's no such thing.

If I'm being completely honest here, I would have to say that I started studying magic out of a sense of curiosity — out of a need to discover and learn something entirely new. I mean, it wasn't as if my life was particularly boring before magic. I had my job, my wife and kids, and Aikido. I had plenty. What I didn't have, I guess, was a new challenge. Magic filled that void.

After I convinced that crusty old magician to serve as my magic mentor, there was no looking back. I dove into my studies. When I wasn't working, hanging out with the kids, or down at the dojo, I was pretty much always working on my magic.

I kept a deck of cards in my pocket. I kept a deck of cards in the bathroom. I practiced palming techniques when I was sitting at my desk, walking down the street, or stuck in traffic. It was a lot of practice and a lot of work. Believe me, magic is not easy.

But you know what? I loved every minute of it, because it never felt like work. It felt exciting. It felt, for lack of a better term, magical. Which, when you think about it, makes complete sense.

When we discover something new in our lives and when we take on a new challenge, new doors of possibility open, new roads and paths appear; in those moments we are, in a sense, reborn. Our brains literally come back alive, buzzing with activity. That excitement of newness is something that we, as humans, really do desperately need. I think this is maybe truer now in the modern world than ever before.

The daily grind of sameness that we all endure — that dulling routine of waking up, eating breakfast, slurping down coffee, fighting traffic, slogging through a work day, battling more traffic on the way home, catching some television time, and then going to bed — doesn't just wear us down, it also wears our brains down.

Our brains are amazing things. They are, scientists say, literally the supercomputers of our lives — supercomputers capable of more than we even imagine. Of course, we have to choose to actually use them.

Just as our bodies need exercise — just as we absolutely need to put our bodies to the test and just break a sweat every once in a while — our brains also need a good workout. You can't retire your brain once you get your college degree; you've got to use it, and keep using it if you want it to serve you well. Get too mentally lazy and your brain will literally atrophy. And, as it shuts down, all of the excitement and beauty will slowly but surely drain right out of your life.

I guess the point of this little rant boils down to this simple piece of advice: Don't let yourself get too comfortable.

Don't take life for granted. Don't let yourself settle for the same-old, same-old. Don't let your world ever become boring, or predictable, or colorless. Don't let yourself stop believing in the magic of this life.

New, wonderful things are out there waiting for you. They really are. *And you have to seize them.* That's what I did when I found magic, and I'm so happy that I did.

See, I thought I knew everything there was to know about life — or, at the very least, all there was to know about my life. I thought I had discovered everything there was to discover. I thought I had become everything that I was going to become. I thought, basically, that my life was set in stone: job, family, friends, and Aikido.

That was it. And that was all there was ever going to be.

Then I found magic.

And in a very small, very personal way, that discovery brought new color — and much-needed new magic — to my world, a world that had maybe gotten just a little too comfortable. I saw things differently. I lived life differently. I started to see that the magic in my life wasn't just tied up in card tricks and illusions; the magic in my life, I realized, was everywhere.

If there's one thing I know for sure: Not everything in this world — not everything in your life for that matter — is as it seems.

Far too often, we walk through our lives with blinders on, so narrowly focused on what's directly in front of us (usually, those little nagging problems of our day-to-day existence) that we can't appreciate the absolute beauty that lies on the periphery.

We wake up in the morning thinking about the mortgage, the electric bill, the leaky faucet in the bathroom, or our worries at work. What we don't think about is the good stuff. Don't forget the roof over your head, the family and friends you have, the opportunities before you, and the life all around you.

And that stuff is always there — every day. Even on the bleakest Tuesday morning, in the dead of winter, when money is tight and worries are high, I promise you that there is beauty in your life. There is magic in your life.

And this magic is powerful, powerful stuff. It can put a smile on your face. It can put a smile on the faces of those around you. It can get you through the toughest of times, and, it can help you enjoy the best of times even more than you usually would. It can bring color to your world just like it brought color to mine.

No, the magic won't solve your problems. It will, however, help you endure them. And that's a good thing. Because — and here's a shocker for you — life sucks sometimes.

Sometimes we lose our jobs. Sometimes relationships go bad. Sometimes we get divorced. Sometimes our kids struggle or cry or let us down. Sometimes we let our kids down, too. Sometimes we get sick. Sometimes people die. Sometimes we have to deal with a whole lot more bad than good in this life.

And know what? That's not ever going to change. Because that's life. We are flawed beings living in a flawed world — a world where there really is no fairness. No, life is not "fair." In fact, very often, it's quite unfair. Disasters happen. Layoffs happen. Sickness and death happen. In this life, we are going to be confronted, inevitably, with true misery. It's unavoidable.

So go ahead, take a deep breath and accept that. Accept the reality that not all of your dreams are going to come true. Accept the reality that bad things will happen to you, and to the people you love. Accept sadness as a part of this world.

Then, ask yourself one simple question: Given the fact that life is going be hard, *how are you going to deal with it?*

Are you going to be miserable? Are you going to make everyone around you miserable? Are you going to curl up in a ball and die? Are you going to give up?

Or, are you going to choose to endure?

A few chapters back I told you that you didn't need to be an Aikido master to find the balance in your life.

And, now, I'll tell you this: You don't need to be a magician to find the *magic* in your life, either.

All you need to do to find that magic — to live that magic — is accept that magic exists, and accept magic as a real part of your life, just as you have accepted that sadness is a real part of your life.

To find the magic in your life, you need to act a little bit less jaded. You need to let go of your bitterness or anger, your worries and stress, and your insecurities and jealously. You need to be able to wake up in the morning with the courage to look past life's imperfections and miseries and realize that, yes, you are incredibly lucky to be alive. You need to be wise enough — and perceptive enough — to know that, no matter how young you think you are, and no matter how much time you think you have left, the clock is indeed ticking.

I'm telling you: You simply do not have the time to spend your every waking moment worried, miserable, or angry. You have to understand that if you keep waiting for the perfect day, you'll wait forever; then life will be over and you'll have missed all of it.

No, not every day can be sunny and beautiful, either literally or metaphorically. So just accept that — and accept that a cold, miserable, sleet-riddled day in January counts just as much as those sunny and 70-degree slices of heaven in May. Enjoy those cold, miserable days for what they are: A day to be alive. A day to be nice to those around you. A day to show your kids you love them. A day to grab a beer and have some laughs with your buddies. A day to make the most of your short time here on Earth. A day to do what you love. A day to find your magic.

Here's my point: *You've got to be able to persevere in this life in order to find the magic in your life.*

You've got to be able to find something in this world to get you up and out of bed every day — something that will make you want to attack that day ahead, something that will energize you, excite you, motivate you, and push you.

And whatever that thing is? Well, that's your magic.

For me, the magic is my magic; Aikido; and my kids, my wife, and my friends. That's the stuff I live for. For you, the magic is going to be something else entirely. Maybe it will be gardening. Maybe it will be writing. Or, maybe it will be painting, your job, or your family. Only you can decide what does it for you.

What I want you to do is find your magic — and *live it*. Maybe more specifically, *live for it*.

If your kids are the magic in your life, then make it your mission each and every day to show those kids how much you love them — how you love them more than anything and anyone in the entire world. Pour yourself into your work to give them all the best life has to offer. Be understanding and kind. Be the best parent you can be.

If your spouse is the magic in your life, then be the best spouse this world has ever seen. Bring your wife flowers every night. Listen to your husband's problems — and help him solve them. Think of your spouse first — and yourself second. Make sure they know each and every day that they have been blessed with the greatest, most loving partner for which they ever could have hoped.

If your garden is the magic in your life, then don't dawdle away those weekend mornings paying bills or sitting at your computer sending e-mails that can wait (and yes, they can wait) until Monday. Get yourself up out of bed, keep yourself away from that desk, and go outside into that garden. Pour yourself into that plot. Make it heaven here on Earth. Enjoy every single moment you get to spend working on it, wandering through it, and showing it off to others.

We all have something to be grateful for — something to love — in this life. I do. You do. Everybody does.

That thing, or that person, that you love more than anything else?

Well, that's your magic.

Grab it. Embrace it. Live it.

You'll be happier if you do.

No, magic is not "real."

I am a working magician, and so maybe I shouldn't say this, but I'm going to go ahead and admit this much (brace yourselves): There is not a person on this Earth — not me, not David Blaine, not David Copperfield, not anybody — who actually has the supernatural ability to cut a person in half and then put them back together; or pull a rabbit out of an empty hat; or read your mind; or make the Statue of Liberty disappear.

Wizards don't do wizardry. Sorcerers don't have any actual power. And magicians don't do "real" magic. We're just entertainers.

The card tricks that I perform? Blaine's "levitations?" Copperfield's massive spectacles? All of it is nothing more than sleight of hand. Illusion. Make-believe.

No, magicians are not supernatural, and magic is not "real." Of course, it doesn't make one bit of difference. In reality, people don't love magic because they think magic is "real." They love magic because they love a good mystery. Because they are enamored with the unexplained. Because they really, really want to believe in unseen, impossible powers.

They want to believe that this life, this world and this universe — the Sun and the stars; the trees and flowers; the lakes and rivers; the natural wonders big and small; our friends and families; the things and people we love — are not just some huge coincidence, the result of a massive, completely accidental explosion billions and billions of years ago.

We want to believe there is more to life than meets the eye — more to life than the physicists and cosmologists and chemists tell us there is. Well, I'm here to tell you: There *is* more to life than the physicists, cosmologists, and chemists tell us.

Yes, the universe may be a fluke. Yes, all of the living things in this world may be what they are specifically because of the cruel, cold and inevitable process of evolution. Yes, it's possible that there is no afterlife. Yes, it's possibly even true that there is no real answer to the question that has plagued us for centuries: "Why are we here?"

There are, however, these little facts: We *are* here, and we *are* alive.

Beyond all of the cold realities of life, and of science, there is the *beauty* of life. There are the still-unexplained joys of this world. There is the unquantifiable power of love. There is the immeasurable beauty of a summer afternoon. There is the incalculable value of true happiness.

There is the magic of life — the magic of everyday life — in this imperfect but beautiful world. The magic is not always easy to find. In fact, sometimes it's darn near impossible to find. But it's there; it's always there. And if you want to live a truly balanced life — a life of true mental and physical happiness — you have to find that magic. You have to grasp hold of it, own it, and pass it along to those you love.

CHAPTER 8

The Magic of Misdirection: Finding Balance in New Directions, New Challenges, and New Ideas

I've spent the last seven chapters telling you why balance is so important — and how you can achieve balance in your life.

I've told you about nutrition and exercise, relaxation, and calm. I've told you how to strike that oh-so-delicate balance between work and family. I've also told you how (and where) to find the magic in your life.

I know it has been a lot to digest, but, hopefully, through all of those chapters, all of those stories, and all of those lessons, you've walked away with a better understanding of the most important lesson this book has to offer: A *balanced* life is a *happy* life.

A balanced life is a life that places as much importance on making it home for dinner with the kids as it does on making that big business deal. A balanced life is a life that makes time not only for physical challenges — for pushing yourself to your very limits — but also for peaceful reflection on the beauty of life itself. A balanced life is a life that makes room for a little bit of magic. A balanced life is, in many ways, exactly what it sounds like: A life in which all things — all truly important things, at least — are weighed equally. A balanced life is a life that never tips too far in one direction.

But, before we go any further — before we wrap up this journey we've taken together through all the elements of The Balance Diet, there's one last element we need to explore.

In the previous chapter, we discussed the idea of "magic." Specifically, we talked about how and why it's so crucially important, every single day, to find the magic all around us — the magic of our families, the magic of nature, and the magic of every day on this Earth.

And certainly, that kind of magic is important. It is, after all, the stuff that makes life worth living. However, it is not the only kind of magic out there.

And it's not the only kind of magic that will get you to the mountaintop of The Balance Diet.

There are some people who insist there were only two musicians in the entire 20th century who truly redefined their instruments.

One was Jimi Hendrix, the 1960s psychedelic rock legend who not only topped the charts with a string of timeless hits, but also literally rewrote the rules about how to play the electric guitar.

The other was John Coltrane, the oft-troubled but ridiculously talented jazz player who tore down all preconceived notions about the saxophone — not to mention jazz music as a whole. From his groundbreaking work as a sideman in Miles Davis' legendary late-1950s quintet to his remarkable and unparalleled solo career, Coltrane broke down one musical barrier after another. He invented entire kinds of music. And by the time he died in 1967, at the age of 40 years old, he was already considered a jazz legend.

Now, anybody who knows anything about Coltrane knows that his life was a struggle; a "balanced life," it was not.

He battled drug addiction and alcoholism. He never enjoyed a stable, supportive family life. Depression hounded him. His only release — his only refuge, really — was his music. And given all his myriad problems, maybe it's no surprise, in a way, that the music was so utterly spectacular; all of Coltrane's despair and all of his pain, it seemed, was released through his music. In his frantic, fast-paced playing, a listener might literally imagine Coltrane freeing himself from his demons via his saxophone — words and emotions poured out in musical scales. In Biblical times, they spoke in tongues. Coltrane, you might assume, spoke in saxophone.

But the fact is, it would be quite wrong, not to mention unfair, to assume that Coltrane's music was just a release — to assume, as many new listeners might, that his playing was strictly an improvisational expelling of demons. Because while Coltrane's music might sound improvised, the reality is that nothing this man did happened by accident. Like Davis, his mentor, Coltrane carefully planned and penned each of his recordings; maybe more to the point, he also carefully curated his art — and, by extension, his entire career.

He did so through the smart, timely use of magic — a kind of magic that I call "misdirection."

Coltrane's philosophy about his life — or, at the very least, his philosophy about his music — was fairly simple: He believed that the moment his music became "predictable" was the moment his music would be destroyed. So, well, he never let that happen.

He never let himself get too comfortable. He never made the same record twice. He never let himself fall into a routine. He was always looking for new inspiration, always seeking new challenges and, most importantly, constantly pushing himself — forcing himself — to go where he'd never been. Even places that he wasn't comfortable going.

"When I feel myself moving in a straight line," he famously proclaimed, "I go the other direction."

For Coltrane, the magic of misdirection worked wonders. It kept him on his toes. It kept his life interesting and meaningful. It kept his music fresh and unpredictable. And, notably, it helped him sell a ton of records — both A Love Supreme and My Favorite Things are certified gold, making them two of the biggest-selling albums in jazz history.

This may be oversimplifying things, but it seems to me that what Coltrane did, essentially, was this: He used the magic of misdirection to knock himself off balance — and then found strength, purpose, and meaning in the fight to get himself back in balance.

It was gutsy. Maybe it was even crazy. Regardless of how you see it, for John Coltrane, it worked.

And you know what? It can work for you, too, because I know it works for me.

There's nothing wrong with playing it safe. There's nothing wrong with being responsible. There's nothing wrong with being conservative. There's nothing wrong with saving your money rather than spending, driving a practical car rather than a sports car, or brown-bagging your lunch every day rather than buying one.

Let's face it, playing it safe — taking the conservative and responsible route — is, generally speaking, a very good thing. Heck, if more people played it smart with their money and if fewer people acted so recklessly, the world would probably be a much better place. For example, maybe we wouldn't have had this little financial meltdown that the 2010 economy is currently experiencing.

But I'll tell you what: If you play it safe all the time, you're gonna get bored real quick. You can't always be the responsible one. You can't always be dutiful and buttoned-up. You can't always do things by the book.

And no, you can't always be balanced. Or more accurately, I don't think you *should* always be balanced.

Every once in a while, even a balanced life needs a little jolt, a little spice, and a little excitement. And, that's where the magic of misdirection comes in.

So often in our lives we put our heads down and focus on just one thing so intently — our jobs, our bills, or our health — that we fall into a sort of maniacal, horse-with-blinders-on rut. It's a rut of normalcy and a rut of predictability. One day becomes just like the day before, one week becomes just like the week before, and one month becomes just like the month before. Then the year has passed. Maybe it was a good year. Maybe we did well on the job. Maybe the kids did great in school. Maybe we made great money. Maybe everything was "just fine."

And maybe "just fine" is OK with you. But, if I'm being honest, just fine is not good enough for me.

I happen to believe that we were put on this Earth to do more than just be "fine." I happen to believe there is more to life than "getting by." I happen to believe the moment we let ourselves fall into a routine, and then decide to stick with that routine, is the moment we lose a little bit of the magic in our lives.

I believe that, even when it doesn't feel right — even when the thought of doing something "different" makes us a little bit uncomfortable or a little bit worried — our lives cannot be full, balanced lives unless they are lives in which the pattern of the everyday is occasionally interrupted by the magic of misdirection. To reach our full potential, we must challenge ourselves with new directions, new ideas, and new challenges.

I'm no John Coltrane; I know *that* much. But I certainly understand what that man meant when he said: "When I feel myself moving in a straight line, I go the other direction."

You know why? Because, in my own small way, *I do the same thing*, and it makes a big difference.

There are times when, to my great surprise, I realize that everything in my life is actually working just the way I want it. There are days when the kids are well-behaved and loving and easy; days when my wife and I are getting along wonderfully; and days when sales are strong, when my magic shows are a hit, when my workouts are awesome, and when stress seems to be nonexistent.

You might even call those perfect days. And in a way, they are perfect. I love those days. I cherish them.

But in the back of my head, I know that they simply aren't the norm. Not every day will be a perfect day. Not everything in my life is going to be oh-so-perfect all the time. It's just not possible. So you know what I try to do? I try to convince myself — force myself, even — not to worry myself too much when the days aren't perfect.

As I've said many times in this book already, there isn't anything wrong with working hard. There isn't anything wrong with having a goal and working toward it. There isn't anything wrong with being dogged about achieving our dreams.

However, there is something wrong with spending all of your time worrying about those abstract things at the end of your self-constructed tunnel. There is something wrong with fretting about "perfection." There is something wrong with being so obsessed with "achieving" something that you lose sight of the vast potential for fun — for joy, for laughs, and for old-fashioned good times — that this world has to offer.

And there is most definitely something wrong with living a life so utterly predictable — so focused on the handful of things that you think you need your life to be — that every Monday is the same as the Monday before, every weekend is the same as the past weekend, and every vacation is the same as last year's vacation.

I mean, you've got to live, guys, and misdirection can help you do just that.

It's about a 75-mile drive from my responsible, practical suburban home in Philadelphia to the completely irresponsible, impractical and — let's face it — financially perilous gambling mecca called Atlantic City.

Atlantic City is a place where, above all else, you spend money … and lose money.

It's the kind of place where you might be inclined to have one too many drinks (they are free, after all), the kind of place where you might be persuaded to play one too many hands of blackjack, and the kind of place where you probably are going to spend way too much money on a hotel room — and then regret it when you get the credit card bill next month.

Bad. Atlantic City is just bad. But, it's also *good*. Good in a bad way, of course. But still *good*.

For all of its many faults, Atlantic City also is the kind of place where you can cut loose, relax, and flat-out have a good time. Drinks. Dinner. Gambling. The boardwalk. The beach. I find that a weekend trip to Atlantic City can be downright therapeutic. A weekend trip to Atlantic City offers true escape from the real world — and just enough misdirection to knock me off balance (at least for a couple of days).

Here's an admission for you: As I write this chapter, I am finalizing the details on a weekend trip to Atlantic City — a getaway weekend for my wife and me.

Some how, some way, I lucked into a great rate at the Borgata — easily the nicest and most luxurious casino and hotel down there. And even though (or, possibly, because) life has been so crazy busy lately — work has been crazy, travel has been crazy, and the kids have been crazy — I made the spontaneous decision to take advantage of that great hotel rate. I booked the room and found a sitter. And, in a couple of weeks, my wife and I will be doing the completely irresponsible and impractical thing: We'll be leaving work and stress and everything else behind and spending a weekend in a place where we're almost assured to spend too much money, have too much to drink, not get any exercise, and generally run ourselves ragged.

And you know what? I'm really looking forward to it.

Now don't get the wrong idea here. Don't think that I'm telling you the only way to tap into that "magic of misdirection" is to engage in potentially financially questionable behavior, because that's not the point at all.

My point is this: Every once in a while, even when things are going great — and even when you're feeling as balanced as could be — it's not necessarily a bad idea to throw yourself a random curveball, to challenge yourself to do what you're not "supposed" to do, to break out from the daily routine and just go do something (a little bit) crazy.

Here's a question: How many days have you woken up and just thought to yourself that the day might be better spent on the golf course or taking your son fishing instead of sitting through the drudgery of another day in the office? How many times have you dreamed of taking a completely impromptu vacation to the Bahamas — just dropping everything, packing a bag, and hopping on that plane? Or, packing everyone in the car to take a nice day trip? Or, surprising your wife by coming home early, taking her to a luxurious lunch, and buying her something nice?

My guess is you've had these thoughts at least a dozen of times, if not more. But, I'm also guessing you've rarely followed through on those thoughts.

That seems pretty sad to me, and I'm sure it seems pretty sad to you, too. It's sad not to have the courage to do that kind of stuff every once in a while. It's sad to be scared to live your life. It's sad to be scared of misdirection.

And it's especially sad to think that you might live your entire life without understanding just how beneficial that magic of misdirection can be — and not just in the moment when you're living that misdirection, either.

The fact is, the magic we find in misdirection stands to benefit us, and enrich our lives, long after the thrill of the misdirection itself has passed.

That's why misdirection — the very element of The Balance Diet that can knock us off balance — is nonetheless essential to, in the long term, keeping us in balance.

Here's what John Coltrane understood: He understood that in misdirection — in randomness — we could find inspiration. He understood that by throwing ourselves out of focus, we could regain our focus. He also understood that by throwing ourselves out of balance, we could find our balance once more — and a stronger balance at that.

Though we may think otherwise, the fact is that who we are, what we do, and how we live is not set in stone. It's not predetermined. There's no such thing as "fate." We control how lives unfold. We control what we achieve. We decide how we live. And, we have the power, every single moment of every single day, to completely change who we are — to transform ourselves utterly and completely, from where we live and who we love to what we do and how we are defined.

For John Coltrane, misdirection — consciously making the choice to change direction when he feared life was becoming too easy, or his art was becoming too predictable — served as a means of survival. It kept his art vibrant and fresh. By extension, it kept his bank account healthy. And, we can assume, it also kept his life, for all of its troubles, worthwhile and beautiful.

For us, misdirection need not be so dramatic. For us, misdirection might be as simple as dropping a bad habit — or taking up a new hobby. For us, misdirection can be deciding, simply for the heck of it, to begin training for a marathon, to take flying lessons, or to go skydiving. Misdirection can be becoming vegetarian or, after years of vegetarianism, deciding to go back to eating meat. Misdirection can be leaving your job, starting a new career, or moving across the country.

Or, misdirection can be as simple as waking up on a Monday with a plan in place — then scrapping that plan entirely and doing something altogether different. Something unreasonable. Something impractical. Something a little bit crazy. Something that your boss probably wouldn't like but your wife and kids would love — and cherish.

So, take the plunge. Tomorrow morning when you wake up, do the precise thing you don't think makes any sense. Dive into it. Don't question yourself. Live that moment for all its worth. Immerse yourself in misdirection. Embrace the challenge and the disorientation.

Because maybe you'll discover something while doing so that will completely change the way you look at your life. Maybe your escape — your submission to the magic of misdirection — will actually change the way you live your life.

Or maybe the changes won't be quite so dramatic at all. Maybe the magic of misdirection will do no more than simply make you grateful for the life you do have. Maybe the magic of misdirection will reinforce to you that all that you had believed previously really is what you believed.

Or maybe, just maybe, the magic of misdirection will serve the simple purpose of knocking you off balance — just off balance enough, that is, to make you appreciate the balance you had achieved before.

CHAPTER 9

The Importance of Patience En Route to Balance

Patience.

That's a word I want you to keep in mind now that we've covered all of the elements of The Balance Diet — and now that, presumably, you are ready to begin your own pursuit of a balanced life.

You absolutely must have patience — with yourself; with your friends and family; with your boss; with your employees; and pretty much everyone with whom you come into contact; and with life in general.

Here's the reality: Achieving balance, and living balance, is not easy. It will not happen overnight. It will not happen without a whole lot of work. And it will most definitely *never* happen if you allow yourself to get too frustrated, too soon, because of the all-too-inevitable challenges you're going to face along the way.

My advice is simple: Don't be too hard on yourself. Don't expect too much too soon. Don't expect to wake up tomorrow and have everything fall into place, just as you'd always hoped it would. Don't believe that simply hoping for a balanced life is going to get you a balanced life. Because that's just not how it works. Not for me. Not for you. Not for anybody.

In all honesty, I really do believe this book can help you live better. I really do believe that this book can help you live happier. And, I really do believe that this book is chock full of lessons that can make a difference in your life.

But, I absolutely do not believe that *just* reading this book is going to solve all of your problems, make all of your worries go away, and make all of your dreams come true.

I don't believe that even a little bit.

So, don't look at this book as some kind of panacea. There's no such thing. Don't look at your completion of this book as some kind of transformative life event. Instead, in the moment that you finish the last sentence of this book — in that moment you decide that a balanced life is the kind of life you want to live — I want you to realize that you have done nothing more than just taken the first step of what is almost certain to be a long, difficult, challenging, and ultimately very, very rewarding journey.

This book is the beginning, not the end — not even close to the end.

In short, before you finish this book and before you begin the hard work ahead, I want you to both rejoice at your realization that a better life is out there, and temper your enthusiasm with the knowledge that attaining that life is going to require effort, time, dedication, faith, and, of course, patience.

A whole lot of patience.

Life gets in the way of balanced living.

That's as true a statement as there is in this book.

So let me assure you, there are going to be days for you when the very idea of achieving and living a balanced life is going to seem impossible or even ridiculous. There are going to be days (or weeks, or months) when your job is simply going to demand more of your time than you'd like. There are going to be days when your boss won't get off your back. There are going to be times when those unforeseen events that make life so unpredictable (and, it should be noted, interesting) are going to toy with your emotions, dominate your perspective, and, ultimately, throw you off balance.

There will be times of depression and sadness — and times of joy and happiness. There will be accidents and injuries and illnesses and divorce, but there will also be new jobs, new love, and new babies.

Life is going to be as complicated and beautiful and frustrating and unpredictable as ever, and no matter what it throws at you, you're going to have to deal with it. Ideally, you will be able to do so and still keep your life in balance. But, more than likely, life is going to occasionally get the better of you.

As humans, we are programmed to be (overly) emotional beings, which means that we can be deeply affected — not just emotionally, but also physically — by the twists of fate that shape our lives. That's what makes us human, after all. We are prone to enormous joy and dark depression, festering anxiety and boundless hope. We are quite simply not immune to our own emotions.

We are, in many ways, not built to be balanced. So, a lot of times, *you're not going to be balanced.* And you know what? That's OK.

Here in the real world, nobody is perfect. And, none of us — not even my great mentor, Shuji Maruyama Sensei, the man who taught me more about balance than any other — are ever going to achieve permanent, perfect, enduring balance, either. It is quite simply an impossible dream to live in such a state.

But that's not important. It really isn't.

I've never once in this book suggested that you need to be perfect. I've never once suggested that I'm perfect, or perfectly balanced for that matter. All I've suggested is that working toward a balanced life can help bring you a better life.

What's important is that we never stop *striving* for that balance. Aspiring to it. Believing in it, and believing that we are good enough to achieve it, if not forever and always, then at least every once in a while.

What's important is that we make the choice to *want* a balanced life, and that we then commit to overcoming our natural, human flaws that stand in the way of us getting there.

It's important that we not succumb to our fears and insecurities. It's important that we not become crippled by anxiety. It's important that we remember to live for the moment — to appreciate and love the beauty of now — even as we plan and work toward a better future.

It's important that we take nothing — not our jobs, not our families, not our friends, not life itself — for granted.

It's important that we remain calm during the storms of life — and make ourselves at peace with the fact that those storms will roll in.

It's important that we remember, no matter what life may throw at us, that happiness, calm, and peace can be achieved — and that these things can be achieved, most easily, through balance.

CHAPTER 10

Do This for Yourself

If you're a perceptive reader, you've probably realized by now that there's one element of The Balance Diet that we have yet to explore. And given that we've already arrived here at the end of the book, maybe you think I've forgotten about that element altogether. I assure you, I haven't.

The element I speak of is selfishness.

This might sound like a bad thing, because, usually, it is. But in the case of The Balance Diet, selfishness isn't all that bad. It isn't bad at all, actually. You see, I'm not talking about your typical selfishness here. Rather, I am talking about a novel idea. The idea is that being selfish is OK — that taking time out of your life specifically to enjoy your life and make your life better is, in fact, a perfectly normal thing to do. In fact, it's a perfectly healthy thing to do.

See, I really do believe that when we achieve balanced lives, we can be better people — more positive, happier, and loving people — for others in our lives. We can be better husbands and wives, friends, and bosses. We can be more fun to be around. We can be more magnetic. More interesting. More positive.

And, of course, this makes life more wonderful for those around us.

But it's important not to pursue a balanced life just for the benefit of others. I want you to pursue a balanced life *for you*. And I want you to understand — to believe, in fact — that wanting something for yourself is just fine, that wanting something for yourself is not something of which you should be ashamed, and that treating yourself to the good life is something that you *should* do. Often.

Successful achievement of a balanced life is going to require you to be just a little bit selfish. And yes, that's perfectly OK.

CONCLUSION

What You Should Take Away from this Book

Before we say our goodbyes, let's review what this book is all about — why I wrote it and what I'd like you to take away from it.

In the Introduction, I wrote about my discovery of the power of a balanced life through a sort of early-life crisis — a time of pain and bewilderment that made me think more deeply about who I was and who I wanted to be. Not to mention what I really wanted out of life.

Granted, in the grand scheme of things, my little high school drama — breaking up with my girlfriend, confronting the reality of my waistline, making the decision to overcome my doubts and insecurities — was probably not that big a deal to anyone but me. And, yeah, to me, it was a big deal. At least, it was enough of a big deal to be a life-changing event for me.

The reality: As minor as that crisis was in the context of the wider world, my little episode set off a chain of events that ultimately led me down the path of happier living — and balanced living.

Because of that crisis, I discovered Aikido and nutrition and fitness. I also discovered that new possibilities — new avenues for enjoying this world — are there waiting for us, every single day. And, I discovered this little truth about life: We can change our lives, whenever we want to, if only we are *truly committed to changing our lives*.

And, I'll keep reiterating the following points: You have the *choice* to be happier, healthier, more loving, more respected, and more balanced. You can lose that weight. You can leave a job that makes you unhappy. You can be a better spouse or parent. You can decide, right now, that you want to live differently — and reap the benefits of doing so. It worked for me, and it can work for you, too.

I truly believe I am a better, smarter, happier, and more balanced person today than I was 20 years back — and that's specifically because I discovered something very special about life (namely, the value of balance) and then committed myself to achieving it.

My journey has not always been an easy one, and there are still days when I battle my own foibles and faults, but there is no question in my mind that I am living a better life today than I ever have before. The reason for my happiness is The Balance Diet.

To me, The Balance Diet — even before I knew that it *was* The Balance Diet — has been the key to my success in business, my happiness at home, and my ability to truly love life, no matter what life has thrown at me. The Balance Diet has helped me endure challenges, tragedies, and failure. The Balance Diet has allowed me to see the beauty in every single day, no matter what the day brings. The Balance Diet has helped me be a better father, a better husband, a better boss, and a better friend. The Balance Diet has made me braver, more loving, more understanding, and more at peace.

The Balance Diet has, quite simply, made me a better person. The kind of person, I hope, that people want to be around.

And, for everything I said earlier — for all of those warnings about how you should not expect to achieve balance either easily or often — all of the work that I've put into my pursuit of balance, and the modest success I've had in achieving it, has not actually been all that backbreaking. If anything, the work has been enjoyable.

Rewarding.

Uplifting.

Inspirational, even.

As my friends and my family will almost certainly attest, there are times when I am most certainly *not* the most balanced person in the world. Sometimes, I let work stress get the best of me. Sometimes, when the kids are crazy, or when I'm tired and worn out, I don't appreciate all of the little things that life has to offer. Sometimes, I don't get my workouts in, don't eat the way I should, and generally let myself fall back into old habits. Sometimes I don't embrace the power of a positive mind. Sometimes, I spend more time worrying than living. Sometimes, I'm just miserable.

But here's the thing: Those "sometimes" don't come along as often as they used to. I am a more balanced person today than I was back in high school, when I was battling my way through college, or during my brief and not-all-that-pleasant stint working at the hospital.

Heck, I am a more balanced person today than I was *yesterday.*

Tomorrow? Well, I expect tomorrow to be even better. Not perfect, necessarily, but better.

And do you know why I believe that? Here's why.

One day at a time. One hour at a time. One meal at a time. One workout at a time. One business meeting at a time. One hug at a time. One *decision* at a time.

My pursuit of balance continues, each and every day, each and every moment.

Are you ready to begin your journey as well?

Let's take a quick look back at the five elements of The Balance Diet.

Element No. 1: The Power of a Positive Mind

Positive thinking, as we learned back in Chapter 4, can be the key to changing the way we view the world — and the way we live our lives.

As Sensei taught us, thinking positive really is half the battle. Because until you believe you actually can do something, you're not going to be able to do it.

In other words, if and when you set goals for yourself — for instance, when you decide that you're going to run a marathon, lose 20 pounds, or write a book — *you absolutely must believe* that you'll accomplish those goals.

Don't let even the faintest doubt creep into your mind. Give yourself a chance. Believe in yourself.

See the world for all of its possibility — not all of its faults. And, see yourself for all of your potential — not all of your shortcomings.

Think positive. Believe.

Element No. 2: Achieving Relaxation and Calmness

As I wrote back in Chapter 6, relaxation and calmness are not only the most important elements of The Balance Diet, but also the most difficult ones.

Our world is fast-paced, highly stressed, and constantly on the move. In the midst of that craziness, however, we must find peace, calm, relaxation, and moments of reflection. We must make the effort to check out from our lives every once in a while. We must realize that, while we tend to obsess about the minutia of life sometimes, there really is a bigger picture out there — a bigger picture that tells a bigger, more important story. We must always remember how lucky we are to be alive in this beautiful world.

We cannot live happily if we cannot relax. We cannot appreciate the beauty of this world if we cannot be calm. And, we cannot achieve balance without relaxation and calmness.

Element No. 3: Living Healthy and Eating Well

These items are self-explanatory. I mean, there's no mystery here.

The mind is a powerful thing. But the mind — our emotional state, and our view of the world and ourselves — is directly influenced by the health of our bodies.

This book is not about physical fitness, per se; as you read earlier, I don't believe that you need to be a fitness superstar to live a balanced life. You don't need to adhere to a strict Vegan diet. You don't need to run 10 miles a day. But, you do have a responsibility — a responsibility to yourself — to treat your body, and by extension, your mind, with respect.

It will pay off. It really will. Find the time to exercise. Make the effort to eat better. You will be happier, better, and, yes, a more balanced person for it.

Element No. 4: Finding the Magic in Your Life

The magic is out there. Your magic is out there.

So, please, go find it.

There is something out there for you — something that will bring color and joy and beauty to your life. It can be a hobby, your religion, a book, a piece of music, or maybe even a career. It can be your family or friends, or your garden out back. It can pretty much be anything, to be honest.

If you've found that thing, you have to embrace it. Commit yourself to it and enjoy it.

If you haven't found it yet? Well, then keep looking, because you cannot be fully happy until you've found your magic. And, yes, you *can* find it. You really can. This world is too big, and too beautiful, to not hold something specifically for you.

Element 5: Be Selfish

Go ahead, guys. Just be selfish. Be selfish about this one thing — being a better you — and you'll be happier for it.

I want you to embrace The Balance Diet for *you*. I want you to live The Balance Diet for *you*. And that's why each of the five elements of The Balance Diet places demands specifically upon, well, *you* — not your friends, not your family, and not anybody else. Just you.

If you want to achieve balance, then it's going to be completely up to you. You're going to have to be the one who puts in the time in the gym, in the dojo, or at the track. You're the one who is going to have to say to yourself, "You know, I need to take 30 minutes, sit outside, and calm myself down for a bit — see you when I'm done." You're the one who is going to have to commit yourself to living your life *joyously*. And, yes, you're the one who is going to need to know when it's time to be a little bit selfish.

In a way, I guess what this book has been trying to say is that it actually takes some *effort* — a good bit of effort, actually — to improve your life. It takes time to be healthier in mind, body, and spirit. It takes real mental commitment to seek and achieve a state of peace and a positive mind. And taking this time and effort? Well, it's going to mean taking some time for yourself. That's just the way it is.

Believe me, I've spent years working toward balance, and if there's one thing I've learned, it's that the moment I stop working at it is the moment that I start to slip up.

We have one shot at life on this Earth, and ours is the one life on this Earth over which we really have control. That's it. Yes, we can be a positive (or negative) influence on those around us. Yes, we can be wonderful parents and loving spouses. Yes, we can be great bosses. Yes, we can become the kind of people who literally light up the room. And when we become these things — when we *are* these things — we have a profoundly positive impact on all of those around us.

But we can only become these things if we are happy, if we are balanced. And, we can only become balanced when we work at it, when we put in the time, when we put in the effort, when we believe in ourselves, and when we decide that we need to be a little selfish — for our own sakes, and for the sakes of those we care about.

I've come a long way since my high school days in Burholme. Yes, I was the fat kid, but I was also so much more than that. I was also unhappy and directionless. I didn't know what I wanted out of life. Maybe more to the point, I didn't know what I could get out of life. I didn't believe in myself. I didn't believe in the world. I was just living day to day, without really living at all. My life had little magic. Little vision. Little excitement.

Then, thanks in part to a few wonderful mentors and thanks in part to my own mental, physical, and spiritual awakening, I suddenly realized there was a lot more to life than I had ever realized.

When I went through that little high school crisis, I was awakened, more than anything else, to the idea of *possibility*. I came to see once and for all that I could be "more." That my life could be "more." That I didn't have to be the fat kid. That I didn't have to be unhappy. That I could do pretty much whatever I wanted. And, by pushing myself to achieve more, I could become a positive influence on others, too. All at once, I bought into all of that.

And today, I'm living a life that, before my awakening, I don't think would have been possible. Not in the least.

At home, I have a beautiful wife and two wonderful children. Our collective goal? To have a blast with life.

Professionally, I have not only found success in sales, and am not only making more money that I had ever dreamed possible back in Burholme, but I've also found fulfillment and excitement and challenge in my "other" career. As a magician, I've found a new passion — not to mention a lucrative and (more importantly) rewarding second career. Through my magic, I am bringing joy to children all across Philadelphia and beyond; I'm also using that magic to teach them about nutrition and helping them build good habits early in life so they never have to endure the challenges I faced, all those years ago, before I woke up.

I've got my problems, sure. Some days are better than others. I am not without my challenges.

But more often than not, do you know how I feel?

Lucky.

Happy.

Balanced.

Blessed.

Sometimes I sit back and wonder at how far I've come. How much I've changed.

There were times in my life when I literally had no confidence in myself. And during those times, I'm quite certain I wouldn't have even believed it possible that I could one day have a home, a wife, and two children; now I do. I wouldn't have believed it possible that I could one day become a fifth-degree blackbelt in Aikido; now I am. And, I certainly wouldn't have believed that I would be so confident — so comfortable in my own skin — that I could get up on stage in front of hundreds of people (thousands, even) and teach *them* how to live happier, fuller, more balanced lives. But today, that's exactly what I do.

And you know what? I love every moment of it. I love being on stage. I love the spotlight. Simply put, I love it because I like who I am — and I love my life.

I want you to like yourself, too. I want you to love your life, too. Having gotten there myself, having climbed the mountain and changed myself for the better, I can tell you, the journey makes living so much more rewarding, much more exciting and fun, and much more beautiful.

We are all dealt a hand of cards in this life. And you can say that some folks' hands are better than others. My response to that: *So what?*

At the end of the day, we've all got our challenges to overcome. Some of us have physical disabilities. Some of us grow up poor. Some of us face sickness. Some of us feel unloved. Some of us are just the fat kid.

But we also have the choice to overcome those challenges. All of us have the opportunity to live a better life — if only we give ourselves the chance. All of us really can achieve the one thing that I believe we all want in this world: A healthy, happy, balanced life.

A good life.

I've got my good life.

Now put down this book, embrace The Balance Diet, and go get yours.